SMOKEY
AND THE
OATMEAL MAN

SMOKEY AND THE OATMEAL MAN

•

Bev Sexton

AVALON BOOKS
THOMAS BOUREGY AND COMPANY, INC.
401 LAFAYETTE STREET
NEW YORK, NEW YORK 10003

PRINTED IN THE UNITED STATES OF AMERICA
ON ACID-FREE PAPER
BY HADDON CRAFTSMEN, BLOOMSBURG, PENNSYLVANIA

To Robbie and Joey—all my love

Chapter One

A cloud of dampness hung over the interior of Vinny's Health Club as masses of overexerted bodies pulled and stretched muscles that were throbbing in protest. Smokey Bates watched in misery from her perch on a stair-stepper. Sweat was dripping steadily in her eyes, but she knew if she stopped long enough to walk to the locker room and grab her forgotten headband, she'd never return to finish her workout. She stared ahead dully, swiping the sweat once every four steps, and trying to talk herself into continuing on the three steps in between.

She hated regimented, mechanical exercise. Especially today, when the endless swiping kept her from drifting off into her usual dreamworld. *Whatever happened to the good old days?* she asked herself. *Every year it gets harder to keep my body from turning into a quivering blob. I want to be sixteen again, when just*

1

existing was exercise. Now all she could think of was a steaming pepperoni pizza. Smokey stomped on the pedal in frustration.

"There you are!" Smokey's friend, Danielle, appeared in front of the machine of torture, looking fresh and perky as usual. "Why are you hiding in here?"

"Couldn't stand another minute of MTV," said Smokey. "Thought I'd try the weight room today. I had hopes that the body builders would be more entertaining than gyrating rock stars."

"Hmm, I see what you mean." Danielle was studying the grunting men in their shorts and muscle shirts. "So that's why they put these step machines in here."

"I guess. But these guys are so wrapped up in themselves and their pecs and abs that they're more boring than MTV." Smokey sighed. "Life just isn't fair, Danielle."

"Having a bad day, are we?" said Danielle, jumping on the empty stair machine beside her friend. "Well, I may just have something to cheer you up."

"It better be good. Because it's not going to be easy," said Smokey ominously.

Danielle hopped off the stair machine and removed a piece of paper from her gym bag. "My friend April gave me this," she said, waving the slip of paper in front of Smokey's face. "And it could be the key to your future."

"April's the one who works at the Tri-Arts Talent Agency, isn't she?" Smokey was suddenly alert.

"Yep. And this is a memo she fished out of the wastebasket. Private and personal. Don't you want to know what it says?"

"I've had my application in at Tri-Arts for months. If that note doesn't say 'Hire Smokey Bates immediately,' it probably won't help much."

"It might as well say that, because this little piece of paper is going to give you the inside track on becoming the editorial assistant to Paul Girard, the hottest agent at Tri-Arts."

"How so?" said Smokey, grabbing for the memo.

"Not so fast," said Danielle, clutching the paper to her heart. "First you have to swear that if you get this job, you're going to find me an agent, preferably Mr. Girard himself."

"I swear," said Smokey wearily. "Now let me see the memo."

Danielle handed it to her, then watched anxiously as Smokey scanned the page.

To: Donovan
From: Paul
Re: Editorial Assistant
I don't want to repeat the Tiffany
experience. It may be difficult, but try to
screen applicants to find the appropriate
marital status.

"I don't get it," she said after reading it over twice. "Who is Donovan? And who is Tiffany?"

"Donovan is the head of personnel. Tiffany is the editorial assistant they just fired. She was beautiful, single, and she dated everyone in the office, and most of the client list. Paul Girard is one of those rare Hollywood types who is happily married and expects his employees to behave themselves.''

''So he's looking for an ugly assistant?''

''Close.''

''Thanks for thinking of me,'' said Smokey dryly.

''Boy, you are in a bad mood. I said 'close.' Guess again.''

Smokey read the memo again. ''He's looking for a married assistant?''

''Bingo. But they can't come out and ask the applicants. That's discrimination.''

''I still don't get it. I've been divorced for five years, and not a prospect in sight. So what's this got to do with me?''

''Do you still have a wedding ring?''

''No. I think I threw it in the trash. It was turning green.''

''No matter. You can buy another one.''

Smokey looked at Danielle as if she had lost her mind. ''Are you nuts?'' she said.

''Do you want the job or not?'' said Danielle. ''You've finally got the inside track on a job that is exactly what you've been looking for. You've got the degree from film school. It's time you put it to use. Waitressing at the Wayside Café is hardly a good use of your education.''

''So I walk in there and lie to them . . . tell them I'm married. That's the inside track?''

Danielle shrugged.

The buzzer sounded on Smokey's stair-stepper, telling her she'd completed her hour of torture. ''I'm going to do the bicycle," she said. "Meet me in the dressing room when you're finished."

"It'll be a while," said Danielle. "I've got an appointment with the new trainer. He's gorgeous, and he's going to help me set up a weight-lifting program."

"Again? You've auditioned every new trainer they've hired, and you still don't use the weights."

"Yeah, but have you seen this guy? He's really gorgeous."

Smokey shook her head as she walked to another corner of the large room and climbed on a vacant stationary bike. She pedaled slowly, thinking about what Danielle had told her. It had been six months since Smokey finished her degree at UCLA's film school, and she had yet to get even a nibble on a job in the movie industry.

She had written three screenplays while she was taking classes, and was working on a fourth, but so far she had no success in finding someone to even read her work. One of her professors at UCLA told her that the best way to get in the business was to find a job, no matter how menial, and work her way up. Once she got inside the industry, he said, she would meet people, and they would know people who would know people, and so on and on. That was the way the movie business worked.

So far the only industry contact Smokey had made was Danielle, a would-be actress. They lived in the same apartment complex and struck up a conversation by the pool the first week Smokey moved to California, and they hadn't stopped talking since—or at least Danielle hadn't.

Danielle was one of the thousands of beautiful young actresses seeking fame and fortune in Hollywood, but so far all she had gotten were commercials and some small speaking parts on daytime TV. Still, Danielle truly believed that success was just around the corner, and Smokey had yet to see her spirits down.

Danielle maintained an active social life and was out most nights with her "man of the week," while Smokey sat home, sweating blood over her latest work-in-progress. Danielle's positive attitude was sometimes the only thing that kept Smokey from quitting her waitressing job, packing her bags, and moving back to Iowa.

While Danielle was happy-go-lucky, she was also on occasion outrageous, and this was one of her wildest schemes yet. *Oh, well,* thought Smokey. *I probably won't get the job anyway, so I guess it won't hurt to invent a phantom husband for the interview.*

Danielle waved from across the room where she was talking to one of the best-looking men Smokey had ever seen. And she was only seeing him from the back. He was wearing shorts and a tank top, and he was muscular but not overbuilt like many of the other guys at the gym. Soft, clean brown hair curled around his head, shorter than most, but long enough to be stylish.

This must be the new trainer, thought Smokey, as the man turned to look at her. He had just a hint of a smile on his face as he caught Smokey's eye, and he appeared to be drawn to her, like he was unable to pry his startling blue eyes away. It wasn't one of those macho, male, appearance-scanning looks, but more like a soul-searching, I-want-to-get-to-know-you-better gaze.

Smokey's foot slipped off the pedal of the bike and she lost her balance for a moment as he continued to stare. Blushing, she caught herself and struggled to get back into the rhythm of the ride. She kept her eyes on the pedals, refusing to let him see how embarrassed she was. When she finally did look up again, he was busy helping Danielle with the hand weights.

Smokey knew most of the guys who worked at the gym on a casual basis, and she occasionally visited with some of the regular bodybuilders. Rarely did the conversations go beyond the day's workout. Smokey loved books and film and the world beyond the gym, but for these guys, muscles were their lives. And many of them had muscles for brains, so she had very little in common with them. Her daily workout was always torture, so it was difficult for her to understand their obsession with weight training.

This new guy was no doubt the same, but Smokey sensed a little more substance to him. He definitely had a well-toned physique, and he moved as gracefully as a cat, not with the swaggering, muscle-bound roll of the overdeveloped hulks. She watched as he worked with Danielle, and he seemed very intent on helping her do the repetitions correctly. He wasn't joking around and flirting with her like the other trainers did.

Smokey couldn't stop watching the workout scenario in front of her. The new guy was really putting

Danielle through her paces, and Smokey had to suppress giggles as her friend broke out in a real sweat. *Nice to see her have to really work out for once,* thought Smokey.

Half an hour later, Smokey was just hanging up the pay phone in the women's locker room, when Danielle came dragging in.

"That guy graduated from the Acme School of Torture," she said, blowing a stray lock of blond hair off her forehead. "Every muscle is screaming. I'm going to the Jacuzzi. Come with me?"

Smokey was bursting to tell Danielle her news, so she changed into her swimsuit quickly and hurried into the pool room.

"Ahhh." Danielle sighed as she sank down into the swirling jets until only her head was above water. "I may never walk again."

"Tough workout, huh?" said Smokey, stating the obvious, while struggling to keep the smirk off her face.

"That Hank's a maniac," said Danielle, her green eyes wide.

"Hank? As in short for Henry?"

"I guess so," said Danielle. "He wants to be a personal trainer. Says there's a lot more money in that. If I had the money, I'd hire him."

"I thought you hated him."

"No. I mean, if I loved the workout, it probably wasn't any good. That was the best one I've ever had. You should schedule a session with him."

"Maybe someday. I've got other things to worry about right now."

"Like?"

"Like an interview with Tri-Arts tomorrow. Paul Girard's office."

"You're kidding!"

"Just got off the phone with them. Three o'clock tomorrow afternoon."

"Hallelujah!" Danielle was shouting and kicking water all over the floor.

"Guess I didn't work you hard enough," said a male voice approaching from behind. Hank the Hunk had a broad smile on his face as he walked toward the pool, his eyes once more fastened on Smokey. "I thought you'd be too wiped to kick like that for a few days."

Smokey was not often self-conscious, but this guy was checking her out more thoroughly than most. She was very much aware of the old, worn swimsuit she had grabbed out of her locker. And although she hadn't gotten her hair wet, she knew it was curling up in a bushy mess from the steam in the room. She sat stone-still hoping for this moment to pass, and vowing never to wear this swimsuit again.

"That workout was nothing," said Danielle, flashing her wide grin and flirty eyes at Hank. "I could do another one right now."

"Okay," said Hank. "Let's go."

"Well, maybe after a couple of hours in here," said Danielle.

They all laughed as Hank hunkered down on the

edge of the pool beside Smokey. "I'm Hank Hudson," he said, extending his hand.

Smokey stared at the hand for a few seconds. She had a thing for men's hands, and this one was perfect. Strong, very wide and muscular, nails neatly groomed and clean.

"Something wrong?" said Hank, breaking her spell.

"Oh, no," said Smokey, blushing furiously. She took his hand tentatively, then quickly drew back. "I'm Maureen Bates. Everyone calls me Smokey."

"Smokey? That's an unusual name for a redhead," said Hank.

"My parents wanted to call me Mo, and it came out sounding like Mokey. Smokey was the obvious next step, and it just stuck."

"Cute," said Hank.

Suddenly, Smokey felt childish, and silly, and even more self-conscious. *You don't even know this guy,* she told herself. *Why are you letting him make you so uncomfortable?*

"Smokey's got a great job interview tomorrow," said Danielle. "We were just discussing her plans."

"Oh?" said Hank. "What do you do?" He was again studying her with great interest.

Smokey glanced at Danielle with a frown, but her friend was grinning, eyebrows raised as she pointed to Hank. Smokey knew what she was trying to do, but she didn't want to share her secrets with this stranger.

"I'm an aspiring screenwriter, but I'd like to get into production, maybe directing someday," she said, deciding not to mention her current employment as a waitress at the Wayside Café.

"And she's interviewing with Paul Girard at the Tri-Arts Agency," said Danielle.

This time Smokey shot her friend a very nasty look.

"Well, I'm impressed," said Hank.

"Don't be," said Smokey. "It's only an interview. *I* called *them.*"

"But Smokey, why don't you tell him about the you-know . . ." Danielle just didn't seem to get the message.

"I don't believe in discussing these things ahead of time," said Smokey, speaking directly to Danielle. "It might jinx the interview."

The three of them sat silently as Smokey continued glaring at Danielle. Fortunately, Hank's next appointment arrived at that moment, and he looked grateful to escape from the uncomfortable scene.

"You could have let him in on it," said Danielle an hour later. They were sitting across from each other at the Ice Cream Palace, eating hot-fudge sundaes.

"What? You think I should have asked him to marry me so I wouldn't have to lie at the interview?"

"Well, you're going to need a husband, and he's not dating anyone."

"How do you know that?"

"I asked him."

"You're impossible, Danielle. He probably has a steady girlfriend."

"Somehow I don't think so." She grinned at Smokey. "Do you, honestly?"

"No," said Smokey, blushing.

"Of course not. Otherwise he wouldn't act so interested in you. Don't tell me you didn't notice. It's time you found a boyfriend. Enough of this sitting home every night of the week."

"It's my only time to write."

"You've got to have some experiences to write about, and you're not going to get them sitting at home every night."

"And I'm going to get experience dating an exercise trainer from the gym? No, the experiences I'm looking for are outside that shallow world. And besides, I want to meet the movers and shakers of the film industry. I want more than muscle-bound cute . . . and hamburgers at McDonald's."

"Hank Hudson is not going to be a small-time trainer all his life. I guarantee it. He's very serious about his future. I think he deserves a closer look. There's more to him than you're seeing."

"Maybe. But right now, I've got this interview to worry about. What should I wear?"

"A wedding ring, for one thing."

"Right. Do you have one I could borrow?"

"Fat chance," said Danielle. "Go to a discount store and buy a cheap band. If you don't get the job, take it back the next day. Tell 'em the jerk left you at the altar."

"Or that I ate too many hot-fudge sundaes and my fingers swelled up," said Smokey, digging for the last drop of fudge in the bottom of her dish.

"Sounds more believable," said Danielle dryly.

"What have you got to wear that's professional-looking?"

"I bought a black suit a couple of years ago. It fits like a dream. Too serious?"

"The man's looking for an employee who doesn't flirt. I don't think you can get too serious. Besides, it's hard enough to make you look grown-up with your red hair and freckles. Black is the only answer."

"Come home with me and help me put this together."

By midnight, Smokey and Danielle had eaten a large pepperoni pizza and two containers of Ben & Jerry's ice cream, but they had Smokey ready for her big moment.

"Do I look fat?" asked Smokey, standing in front of the full-length mirror.

"Stand up straight. Throw your shoulders back. Look confident. Ah, perfect."

They had done Smokey's unruly hair up in a knot on top of her head. Danielle had powdered and painted over the freckles, and the black suit gave Smokey an elegant aura.

"You're going to get this job. I can just feel it," said Danielle, giving her friend an excited hug.

"Thanks, Danielle. Can you come over tomorrow and help me put this all together again?"

"Are you kidding, Smoke? I'm going with you!"

Smokey looked at her friend in horror.

Chapter Two

Danielle was already seated in the office waiting room when Smokey entered. After giving her name and exchanging a wink with Danielle's friend April, the receptionist, Smokey sat uncomfortably in the chair next to Danielle, the only seat available in the busy room. She could not help overhearing the whispered girl-chatter Danielle was carrying on with a young woman who was waiting her turn for an interview with the famous Mr. Girard.

"It's so hard to meet a really nice guy in this business," Danielle was saying, inspecting her manicure. She looked up at the other woman. "Are you married?"

The young woman shook her head. "No way. I want to get my career started first."

Smokey tried to hide her smile as Danielle moved on to her next victim to ferret out her marital status.

Half an hour later, the room was empty except for the two of them. Every time one of the candidates emerged from the inner office, she gave a friendly wave to Danielle.

"How long have you been here?" whispered Smokey, taking a chair across from her friend.

"Since I left you at the store picking out your wedding band. I think I've met most of the applicants. They're all single. You've got this job wired, trust me."

Another woman entered the reception area and Smokey quickly started studying the magazine she was holding in her hand. As the new applicant turned to take her seat, April called out Smokey's name.

"Knock 'em dead," whispered Danielle, her eyes on her next target.

Smokey stood straight and tall, smiling with confidence as she left the room, and Danielle's earnest conversation, behind her.

"Well, finally," said the woman seated at a desk inside the door. She was looking pointedly at the ring on Smokey's finger.

"Beg your pardon?" said Smokey.

"Never mind." The woman plucked a folder from a small pile and handed it to Smokey. A second, much larger, stack of rejected folders was balancing beside the first. "Here's your résumé and application. Just take it with you into Mr. Girard's office. He's waiting for you."

Smokey tentatively pushed open the door the woman had indicated. The office was huge, with gray plush carpeting and lots of wood and green plants. Smokey's eyes focused on a man and a woman standing by a massive desk, talking animatedly.

The man was the most immaculately groomed person Smokey had ever seen, from the top of his perfectly styled hair to his European tailored suit and monogrammed silk shirt with solid gold cuff links, down to his gleaming Italian leather shoes. The woman, too, was dressed expensively, but her stylish suit with matching accessories looked out of place on her, like the clothes were wearing her, rather than the other way around. Her elaborate upswept hairdo was sprayed in place like a helmet, brittle and severe like the grim set of her face.

"Come on in," said the man, walking toward her, hand extended. "I'm Paul Girard, and this is Milly Edwards, my personal secretary." Milly nodded, but said nothing.

"Have a seat while I look at your papers," said Mr. Girard, after glancing at the third finger of her left hand. Smokey noted that Milly, too, was checking out her ring.

Smokey tried not to squirm as Paul Girard leafed through the folder and Milly stood scrutinizing her from head to toe.

"I see you graduated from UCLA film school. That's good. It should help you understand what we do here. I suppose you have a screenplay or two you want someone to read?"

Smokey nodded, blushing.

"Just keep in mind that you're here to work with proven writers. We want to make their lives easier, and that does not include asking them to read your amateur efforts.'' Paul Girard smiled at the flash of disappointment that passed over Smokey's face. ''That doesn't mean that you won't have a chance. You will be learning all the basics of the world of film and Hollywood. It's hard work, but you'll have a better education than you ever could have earned in a college classroom.''

Smokey nodded excitedly. She wanted this job so much. *Please, please, let them pick me,* she silently prayed.

Mr. Girard launched into a history of the company, centering on his personal accomplishments. Finally, he turned to Milly. ''I think you have some questions, Ms. Edwards.''

Milly Edwards preened like an expensive cat as she directed her sharp eyes at Smokey. Speaking in clipped tones, she asked Smokey about her typing and shorthand skills.

Although Smokey had no shorthand, and only minimal typing ability, she brushed over them, explaining that she was a bit rusty, but was certain that she could bring them up to speed once she started using them. She silently thanked Danielle for instilling in her the ability to give appropriate answers, and prayed they wouldn't give her a written test.

Paul Girard was one of those people who liked to hear the sound of his own voice, and Smokey sat patiently while he continued to drone on about his many talents. Milly Edwards was watching her closely through all this, so Smokey made certain she kept an interested smile on her face.

Danielle was no longer in the reception area when Smokey finally emerged. She checked her watch, and discovered she had been in the interview for almost an hour, far longer than any of the other candidates. That had to be a good sign, she told herself, although she had been given very little opportunity to speak. She wondered what Paul Girard could possibly know about her after the one-sided interview. *But maybe knowing I was married was all he needed,* she thought.

Danielle was already working out with Hank when Smokey arrived at the gym. They waved her over to the weight area before she had a chance to climb on the stair-stepper and avoid the inquisition.

"How'd it go?" asked Danielle, gasping as she lifted two large hand weights above her head.

"Pretty good, I think. Of course, I was the only married candidate they had."

Hank chuckled, and Smokey looked at him questioningly.

"Danielle told me all about it," he said, still smiling.

"Thanks, Danielle," said Smokey sarcastically.

"Like it or not, you've got to have a husband." Danielle grunted. "And I think Hank here would be a good candidate."

"Danielle!" Smokey was blushing furiously. "I apologize for her," she said to Hank. "Of course, this is all a joke. If I need a husband, rest assured I can find one on my own."

"I have no doubt about that," said Hank, his warm

eyes bathing her with sympathy. "I'm certain some-one as beautiful as you has the guys standing in line."

"Well . . . I . . . thank you." Smokey was stammer-ing both out of embarrassment and gratitude for his kindness. A warmth she hadn't felt in a long time spread through her, and for a moment she was para-lyzed by his eyes. She looked down as he placed his hand on her arm in a comforting gesture.

How would that perfect hand feel if I held it? she wondered. She had to grit her teeth to keep from ask-ing, from falling helplessly into his arms.

Suddenly, Danielle screeched loudly, a barbell out of control in her hands. Hank broke the spell he had woven as he turned to relieve her friend's distress. Smokey took a deep breath, willing her good sense to return. She turned quickly to walk to the stair-stepper, but she felt Hank's eyes on her back and she knew he was aware of exactly the effect he was having on her.

Smokey had the early breakfast shift at the café the next morning, so it was only two o'clock in the after-noon when she wearily turned the key in her front door, anxious to kick off her shoes and doze in front of the television before starting her nightly writing marathon. The first thing she noticed was the red light on her answering machine, blinking to alert her that someone had left a message.

Smokey didn't get many phone messages, mainly because she didn't know many people, but she always kept the machine turned on, just in case. Someday, she believed, an agent would call with an offer to read her screenplay, and she sure as anything wasn't going to miss it.

"Smokey, this is Milly Edwards," said the familiar, precise voice. "Mr. Girard asked me to call and speak with you regarding the position for which you applied and interviewed. You may return this call at 872-6430." The tape clicked, and a droning, mechanical voice told her that the call had come in at 11:42 A.M.

Smokey stood hugging herself and staring at the machine. As soon as it rewound, she pushed the button a second time and listened to the message again. Then she picked up the phone and dialed Danielle's number.

"Please, please, let her be home," she whispered as the phone rang and rang again.

Just as the message started to play, Smokey heard Danielle's breathless voice over the tape. "Darn," she said, unable to stop the recording. "Hold on a minute." There were a series of clicks and then Danielle spoke again, this time in a charming, upbeat voice. "Danielle Davis speaking."

"It's me," said Smokey. "Where have you been?"

"Out by the pool. What's up?"

"I got the job. I think. I got a message."

"I'll be right there." The phone went dead in Smokey's hand.

They listened to the message together in excitement.

"Call her. Now."

"I need some time," said Smokey, pacing.

"Now." Danielle held out the receiver with one hand, and dialed with the other.

Milly's secretary put Smokey on hold for a few

minutes. "Can you believe it?" said Smokey. "His secretary has a secretary."

"Well, Ms. Bates," said Milly when she picked up the phone. "Mr. Girard has authorized me to offer you the position. You may start next Monday. Is that acceptable?"

"Yes," said Smokey, trying to keep her voice as businesslike as Milly's, while giving Danielle the thumbs-up signal.

"Mr. Girard also asked that you attend a reception on Saturday night at the company headquarters. Tri-Arts is introducing a new client, a screenwriter named Vic Cantrell, and he'd like you to be there. Bring your husband, of course."

"Oh. I'll have to see if he's free."

"On a Saturday night? Well, whatever. We'll see you then."

Smokey's face was pale as she hung up the phone. "She knows. I could tell. She knows I don't have a Mr. Bates."

"Don't be silly. How could she know? What did she say?"

"I have to show up with a husband on Saturday night."

"So we've got three days. We'll figure something out."

Smokey gave her an exasperated look. "I think we need a trip to the Ice Cream Palace," she said.

An hour later, Smokey was on her second hot-fudge sundae.

"You're going to look like a sixteen-year-old with

raging hormones by Saturday night,'' said Danielle, sipping a glass of iced tea, no sugar.

''You're sure you don't know anyone else?''

''All the guys I know are in the business. Chances are they would run into someone they knew, or are known by. It's too risky. Hank's a total unknown. He's perfect for the job, and he's willing to do it.''

''You've already asked him?'' Smokey was horrified.

''Not in so many words. We just talked in general terms.''

''How general?'' asked Smokey suspiciously.

''He just mentioned that he would like to meet some celebrities. Said he needs a job with flexible hours and lots of money, and he'd be a great personal trainer. It's the new 'in' thing for the rich folk. He just needs the opportunity to meet some of them.''

''Really? He said that? This would just be a business opportunity for him?''

Smokey was strangely disappointed, and somewhat irritated. And she wasn't sure why. Hank made her nervous when she was around him, but she'd never be interested in someone like him. She wanted a man with a brain, with a real job . . . if she wanted a man at all. And that was the big question.

She'd left a miserable and short marriage back in Iowa, swearing never to marry again. Tim had been her high school sweetheart. It had been a dream match. He was captain of the basketball team while she was head cheerleader. Tim's parents were pillars of the community and best friends with Smokey's parents. They had married after high school and Tim took over management of the family hardware business. Smokey joined the local Junior League and settled in to be the perfect little wife.

It took less than a year for her to realize that she was bored to death with the Junior League, the country club, and most of all, with Tim. When she discovered Tim had a wandering eye for one of the young female clerks at the hardware store, it gave her the excuse she needed to escape from her suffocating existence. She had taken a small cash settlement from the divorce and moved to Los Angeles.

Now, five years later, she had her college degree and a chance at an exciting career. And she'd done it all by herself. Between classes and waitressing, she'd had little time for a social life, but she really didn't miss it.

I'll never again be dependent on someone else for my happiness, she told herself. The brief imprisonment in an unhappy marriage had taught her to be self-reliant, and very careful about getting involved again. And the last thing she needed was a muscle-bound weight trainer who saw her as a way to get ahead.

Well, that plan could work both ways, she told herself. *I need a presentable husband, and hopefully, Hank could clean up to be presentable. He's unattached, willing, and maybe even eager to play this game.* Besides, did she really have any other choice?

They cornered Hank in the training room. "We've got to talk," said Danielle.

"Sure," said Hank. "But one of you has to do some weight-lifting. Make it look like I'm working. The boss gets upset if we're not doing something productive.''

''Smokey?'' said Danielle, grinning at her friend. ''It's your turn.'' She turned and ambled off toward the stationary bikes.

''You could use some upper body training,'' said Hank, examining Smokey clinically.

''What do you mean by that?'' snapped Smokey.

''Your arms, neck, and back. Most women don't take the time to work on these areas, and they really are important. You spend hours on the stair-stepper, but when's the last time you did some stretching exercises, pulling, lifting?''

''Well, I . . . A long time, I guess.''

''Here, take these . . .''

Smokey's hands wrenched down to her knees the second she accepted the small silver weights.

''Too heavy?'' He grinned.

''Of course not,'' said Smokey, straining to lift the bars up to her waist.

''You'll be lifting twice that in no time,'' said Hank, repressing a grin. ''Now stand with your feet apart but in line with your shoulders. Good. Now lift your arms straight out at your sides.''

Within seconds, Smokey was sweating profusely and on the verge of begging for mercy.

''You really are out of shape,'' said Hank. ''You'll have to take it slow, but you'll have this whipped in no time.''

''Let's do something easier so I've got enough breath to talk.'' Smokey was wheezing.

''Over here's one where you can sit,'' Hank said,

indicating a black machine that looked like just another version of an instrument of torture. ''You put your arms in those straps and pull forward and up. I'll lighten the weights and you can take it nice and slow.''

Smokey sank into the leather seat and took deep breaths while Hank fooled with the weights. ''So I got the job at the Tri-Arts Agency,'' she said.

''Congratulations,'' said Hank as he walked around to the front of the weight machine, checking it out. ''Sit up straight.''

''And I sort of lied about being married. I mean, I was married once, and I really don't want to be married again. You're not married, are you?''

''Was married once. Don't want to be married again.'' Hank grinned at her.

''Oh, yeah, you were married? What happened? None of my business, right?'' Smokey saw a flicker of something cross his face. Sadness?

''It's okay. We married too young. It just didn't work out.''

''Is she still around?''

''Nope. She's happily remarried back East. I came out here to start over.''

''Hmm. Interesting.'' *Sounds like we're acting out the same script,* thought Smokey. *But perfect. We don't need any ex-spouses hanging around, causing problems.*

''So you told them you were married. . . .'' said Hank.

''Yeah. And now I need a husband for Saturday night. There's a reception for a new screenwriter. Just a couple of hours. I mean, I'd understand if you're busy. I could probably find someone else. It's just that I need someone who doesn't know anyone in the industry. And we couldn't think of anyone else. But if you've got something better to do, don't worry about it. . . ."

"I'll go. Now start moving those arms. I'm going to add more weights."

"You'll go? Just like that?"

"Sure. Just let me know the time and place and I'll be there."

"Great. Now you understand, this is strictly business. I mean, I can't pay you or anything, but . . ."

"Look, Smokey," said Hank, standing directly in front of her and glaring directly into her huge brown eyes. "You don't have to worry about me having any expectations about you. I don't have the time, or the money, to get involved with any woman at this point in my life. I'll be happy to help you out, and maybe make some contacts that will help *me* out, but don't expect any more from me. Now let's finish up on that pulley over there, because I have another appointment in ten minutes."

"Can you believe him?" said Smokey to Danielle an hour later when they were on their way home. "What an ego. Who does he think he is?"

"Someone who is doing you a favor. He's the most genuine, honest guy I've met out here, Smokey. I think you're lucky to get him to play the role."

"I guess." Smokey was feeling tired and irritated. And her arms ached.

"So, do you think you can pull it off? Think you can act like old married folks, even though you hardly know each other?"

"Hank suggested we get together early tomorrow morning and exchange life histories. He said we should write things down."

"Good idea. But why early morning?"

"It's the only free time he has. We're meeting at the Coffee Bar. I wonder what he does with all his time."

"He's got you curious, doesn't he?"

"No, of course not."

"Maybe he's got a girlfriend after all. Maybe he's into some illegal activity. Maybe he's a serial killer."

"Danielle! You were the one who got me into this. Don't scare me."

"I'm just kidding you. You worry too much. You've got a great job and a very handsome guy to pose as your husband. You know where he works, so that part's legit. And I'll keep an eye on things, too. Quit worrying so much."

Hank was already sitting in the back booth of the restaurant drinking coffee the next morning when Smokey arrived, a half-hour late. He was wearing worn jeans and a sweatshirt and he looked freshly shaved and scrubbed. He glanced up as she was threading her way through the tangle of chairs and tables. He smiled approvingly at her jeans and crop top. They had never seen each other anywhere but the gym, dressed in anything but workout clothes, and it was like being in a whole new realm. For some reason, it made Smokey feel nervous.

"You're late," he said, checking his watch.

"Sorry."

"How are those arms feeling?" asked Hank, smiling away any irritation with her tardiness.

"Better today. Had to hit the aspirin bottle pretty hard last night."

"You should keep up those exercises. Obviously, you need them."

"Obviously," said Smokey sarcastically.

"Just trying to help." Hank lifted his coffee cup, barely suppressing a taunting grin.

"So did you bring your family history?" said Smokey, deciding small talk was out of the question.

"I was jotting down a few things here." Hank indicated a yellow notepad on the table. "But I was thinking we probably won't have to worry too much about little details. I came out here from New Hampshire; you came from . . . ?"

"Iowa."

"Iowa. Country girl, huh?"

Smokey made a face.

"Anyway, the point is, everyone moved here from somewhere else, usually to get away from something . . . or someone. I think the main thing we have to worry about is our relationship. You know, how we met, how long we've been together, how crazy we are about each other." Hank grinned at her.

"Well, I've written out a complete bio," said Smokey, handing him a sheaf of papers. "The first page is a family tree. You'll notice my family goes back to the first settlers. Not quite the *Mayflower,* but almost. Then I've listed the marriages, children's names, dates, everything you would ever want to know."

"Impressive," said Hank, glancing through the paperwork. "I should have an answer for every possible question if I read all this." He leafed through the papers, then looked up at her with an amused grin. "Do you honestly think anyone will ask?"

"I'm their new employee," said Smokey, blushing. "You never know."

"That's true," said Hank in mock seriousness. "Let's see, you married Tim Phillips seven years ago. The marriage lasted less than two years, no children. How come?"

"I think I knew from the start that the marriage wasn't going to work. And I knew by the end of the first year that I wanted more from life. Not a very healthy atmosphere to bring a child into."

"Do you want to have children?" Hank asked.

"Someday. I feel like I'm just a kid myself. And I've worked too hard to get my career started to give all that up before I've had some success. But I definitely want kids eventually."

"This job is important to you, isn't it?"

"Yes. It's the most important thing that has happened to me. I want to write, produce, maybe even direct. This is the first step."

"Admirable," said Hank in what Smokey felt was a condescending tone.

"And your goals in life . . . ?" Smokey looked at him defiantly. "You want to be a personal trainer?"

"For now, yes," Hank's eyes were amused. "I have a few other goals, but I need money to accomplish them." He was glancing at his watch again.

"I'd love to hear about them," said Smokey politely. *He probably wants to operate his own personal gym,* she thought. *Keep those muscles bulging till the day he dies. And keep the women hovering around.*

"And I'd love to tell you, but I'm already five minutes late for a meeting."

"Oh?"

"Long story. I'll tell you about it later." Hank stood and dropped a couple of dollars on the table. "What time do you want me to pick you up?"

"Pick me up? Well, I guess that would be okay. Let me give you my address." She jotted the numbers down on a napkin. "And I need your ring size."

"Don't bother. I've got a ring." Hank was getting impatient.

"Do you have clothes? I mean . . . like a suit?"

"I can't wear my muscle shirt? How will they know I'm a weight trainer?" Hank grinned mischievously as he made his exit.

Chapter Three

"This isn't going to work," said Smokey, pacing the small living room of her apartment. She was dressed in the always acceptable "little black dress"— simple but exquisitely cut to display her tall, slim figure at its best. Her only jewelry consisted of small pearl earrings. Her mid-length red hair hung loose, tamed for the night in a smooth and sophisticated "do."

"What's not to work?" said Danielle. "It's just a party. You're not going to marry the man." She stopped, looked at Smokey, and burst out laughing.

"Funny," said Smokey. "I just hope he turns up in something presentable."

"Mmm-hmm." Danielle was checking her lipstick in the mirror.

"Speaking of presentable, that's an interesting outfit *you* are wearing."

"Like it?" Danielle tugged at the tight spandex skirt. A colorfully beaded top completed the ensemble. Danielle believed in flaunting her figure.

"That depends," said Smokey. "Where are you going? And who's the man of the hour?"

"Blind date. Going to some party first, then to a new club up in the Hills."

"Hope he can handle it," said Smokey dryly.

"Me, too." Danielle smiled dreamily. "What time is Hank picking you up?"

"In about five minutes, and I'm willing to bet he'll be punctual. He seems to be obsessed with time."

Smokey paused in her pacing for a moment as she heard a loud noise outside in the parking lot. "Someone's got an old clunker of a car. You know, they're letting too many noisy young kids live here."

"Not to mention the paper-thin walls. You can practically hear conversations that go on in the next apartment."

There was a firm knock on her door, and Smokey glanced at her watch. "Three minutes early." She glanced quickly in the mirror, then turned to Danielle. "You don't suppose that car . . . ?"

Danielle shrugged.

Smokey advanced to the door, a frown on her face. But the frown disappeared the minute she saw Hank leaning against the door frame. He was wearing a shirt, tie, and expensively tailored dress pants. The jacket to his suit was slung over his shoulder and held there by the crook of his index finger. This was definitely not an outfit he had picked up at a discount store. Standing there grinning handsomely, he looked like something straight out of the pages of *GQ*.

"Well," she said, "you're here."

"I told you I would be," he said. "You look terrific."

"Thanks. Uh . . . so do you."

"Let's see," said Danielle, grabbing Hank's arm and pulling him into the living room. "Wow. A little too low-key for me, but if you want to ditch this old married woman and hit the clubs with me, I could handle it."

"I'd love to," said Hank. "But I promised the old lady."

"You married guys are no fun," said Danielle.

"Have you got your ring?" Smokey asked, ignoring their comments as she checked him out from head to toe.

Hank patted all his pockets, pretending they were empty before he finally pulled a gold band out of one of them. He slipped it on. "Guess this makes it official. In sickness and in health, as long as we both shall live," he said solemnly.

"Till death, or a better offer, do you part," said Danielle. "Well, I've got to get up to my apartment and put on the finishing touches. You guys have a great time. At least try to pretend you like each other." She waved as she walked out the door.

"Well. I guess we might as well get going," said Smokey, feeling strangely uncomfortable now that they were alone.

"My car's right out here in the parking lot," said Hank, sweeping open the door.

"That's what I'm afraid of," said Smokey, under her breath.

They were silent as they walked the short distance to the parking area. Smokey rolled her eyes as Hank led her to the scruffiest-looking car in the lot. It was a twenty-year-old goldish-tan Subaru and, although it was clean and polished, it had definitely seen better days.

"This is your car?" she asked.

"Yep. Susie Subaru. She's the most reliable woman in my life. Has been for over ten years. And I bought her used."

"No kidding?" Smokey did nothing to hide the sarcasm, but Hank was unfazed.

"She's in mint condition. Need to replace the muffler, but she starts right up every time."

"Look, my little Mustang is parked right over there," said Smokey, pointing. "Let's drive it. I want to be sure I have a ride home."

"Afraid someone's going to see you?"

Smokey looked at him in amazement. How could this guy read her mind? She did want to impress people tonight and she didn't want them to think that the best her "husband" could come up with was a twenty-year-old car. But she was embarrassed to come across as a snob to this perfectly nice man. "Of course not," she said. "I'd just be more comfortable in my own car."

"Of course you would," said Hank. "Are you going to let me drive?"

Although she had many misgivings, Smokey handed over her keys and nervously perched on the passenger's seat. She breathed a sigh of relief a few seconds later as Hank smoothly threaded his way through traffic on their silent drive to the downtown office. *Why does he drive such an awful car?* she thought to herself. *I know he doesn't make a lot of money, but he's so presentable in every other way.* Smokey couldn't shake her puzzlement about this man.

"You won't know anyone tonight," she said. "So just introduce yourself as my husband, and don't offer any information. Let's see, how long do you want to say we've been married?"

Too long, thought Hank, biting his tongue. "A couple of years, I guess," he said. "Don't worry, Smokey, I won't embarrass you." Hank tried to keep the sarcasm out of his voice.

"Thanks," she said absently, wrapped up in her own thoughts and anticipations of the evening ahead. "Vic Cantrell is the guest of honor tonight."

"Should I know who he is?"

"Just the hottest screenwriter to hit Hollywood this year. He's a new client at Tri-Arts."

"Oh."

"I'll be working with people like Vic Cantrell every day." Smokey sighed. "It's so exciting. This is how you get started in the big time. I can't help but think that my destiny is here. I can just feel it."

"Well, don't forget us little people when you're up there with the stars." Hank smiled. Smokey just nodded dreamily.

*   *   *

The reception was just getting started when they arrived. The first person Smokey saw when they walked into the plush reception room was Milly Edwards, scurrying about, checking on the buffet in one corner, talking to the bartender, checking the flowers. Just a tad overweight, Milly compensated by dressing loudly. Although Milly was fairly young, Smokey guessed in her mid-forties, she was overdressed in a sparkling brocade suit. At Tri-Arts, Milly hadn't been very friendly to Smokey so far. And now, for some reason, she was being almost overbearingly chummy.

"Smokey," she called in her fake warm voice. "Nice you could make it. Is this your husband?" Milly was giving Hank the very complete once-over as she advanced toward them.

"This is Hank. Hank, Milly." Smokey smiled absently, her eyes taking in the large room packed with people. She was vaguely aware of the conversation going on between Hank and Milly, but she wasn't paying much attention to the details until Hank slipped his arm around her waist.

"Did you hear that, honey?" he said. "Milly is our neighbor."

"Huh?" Smokey was instantly put on full alert.

"I just moved in to the Sea Palm Court over the weekend," said Milly, beaming. "I didn't realize you guys lived there. Guess if I'd looked on your application . . ." She giggled and batted her eyes at Hank.

"Which building are you in?" asked Smokey, trying to keep the alarm out of her voice.

"First floor, G building," said Milly. "Where are you?"

"First floor, C," said Smokey, mentally calculating locations. "Are you . . . ?"

"Poolside, and you?"

"Poolside," said Smokey, realizing they were located opposite each other across the courtyard that centered around the pool. No doubt Milly could look directly in her windows.

"Well, nice to know I have somewhere to go when I need to borrow a cup of sugar," said Milly, continuing to speak directly to Hank.

As Milly moved closer to him, Hank's grip on Smokey's waist grew tighter and more possessive, and she froze at the growing closeness of his touch.

"Let's go get a drink, shall we, darling?" Hank said, gently moving them away from the hovering Milly. "Nice meeting you, Milly."

"She's a bit much, isn't she?" Hank whispered in Smokey's ear as they approached the bar. Smokey couldn't help but smile at his perception, but she was very much aware of the warmth of his arm, now draped across her back. It wasn't offensive, it was just, well, disturbing.

"I think she suspects something," said Smokey. "The way she keeps asking nosy questions . . . If I didn't know better, I'd think she moved into my apartment complex to spy on us."

"That should be pretty boring stuff, with an old married couple like us."

"Funny," said Smokey. "I think I'll just keep the curtains drawn anyway, thank you. And I think you can take your hand off me now."

"Smokey Bates," a voice boomed from behind

them. They turned in unison to face Paul Girard himself, shadowed by the hungry-eyed Milly. Once again, Paul was perfectly groomed and tailored, but Smokey couldn't help but compare him with Hank. She had to admit that Hank won the style show.

"Welcome to Tri-Arts," said Paul, shaking her hand.

"Thanks, Mr. Girard," said Smokey, reminding herself to breathe.

"And this is . . . ?"

"Oh, sorry. This is my . . . uhmm . . . husband . . . Hank."

"Hank. Nice to meet you. We're pleased to have your wife on board."

Hank smiled and nodded.

"What do you do for a living, Hank?"

"He's a weight trainer," said Smokey. Then she bit her tongue and glanced at Hank in apology.

"A weight trainer, huh? Well, that's an interesting profession. Maybe we can talk some more about it later. Have you ever considered going into film work? I have a feeling you'd project well on camera."

"Uh, no, I really haven't," said Hank, looking uncomfortable.

"There's our guest of honor," said Mr. Girard, glancing at the main door of the reception hall. A short, slender man was posing there while scanning the crowd as if waiting for his admirers to come forward and kneel before him.

"Maybe we can visit later," said Paul Girard, smiling warmly at Hank.

"I look forward to it," said Hank.

Smokey could feel the tension in Hank's arm as it again encircled her waist. "Sorry," she said. "I'm a little nervous."

"I'm sure this little game we're playing will take a lot of practice, but please remember that I'm not a puppet. I am capable of answering questions on my own." Hank was smiling, but his hand was still gripping her firmly as he spoke close to her ear.

"Maybe I'll go over and introduce myself to Mr. Cantrell," said Smokey, removing the possessive hand.

"Good idea. Maybe I'll just stay here by the buffet table and have a chat with the waiter—he's probably the best conversationalist in this whole phony place."

Smokey moved across the room to where Vic Cantrell stood, surrounded by a small crowd. Something caught her attention—a flash of sparkles, a familiar laugh—and she moved up closer to get a better look. Vic Cantrell obviously had someone with him, someone who was causing quite a stir. Then she heard the laugh again, and Smokey pushed through the crowd until she was facing Vic Cantrell's date.

"Danielle! What are you doing here?"

"Dahling!" said Danielle, kissing the air beside her cheek. "So good to see you."

"Cut it out, Danielle. What are you doing with Vic Cantrell?" Smokey pulled her aside and hissed into her ear.

"I didn't know," said Danielle. "My friend April, the receptionist who rescued the memo from the trash, set this up. I'd never met him."

"Remind me to speak with April," said Smokey. "Would you introduce me to your date?"

"Of course, darling," said Danielle, grabbing Vic Cantrell's arm. "Vic, sweetheart. I want you to meet my best friend. . . ."

"I'm Smokey Bates," she said, interrupting the introduction and stepping in front of Danielle. "Besides being Danielle's best friend, I'm Mr. Girard's new editorial assistant."

Vic Cantrell scanned her from head to toe, before kissing her extended hand. "Well then," he said. "Hopefully we'll be seeing a lot of each other."

"Hopefully," said Smokey fervently. Although Vic Cantrell wasn't the type of man she would ever be romantically attracted to, she was consumed with a professional's admiration for his work and his place in the Hollywood scene. Vic Cantrell had everything she wanted. He was living the life of her dreams. With his second successful screenplay in production, he could write his own ticket.

"I admire your work," she said. "I've written some screenplays myself. Maybe someday we can talk about them." Smokey remembered Mr. Girard's warning, but technically she wasn't asking Cantrell to actually read her work.

"Every taxi driver and bartender in this town has written a screenplay," said Vic Cantrell. "But only a few possess true talent."

"And you are certainly one of them," said Smokey, hating to sound like she was gushing, but genuinely filled with admiration for his talent.

"Well, thank you, my dear. We definitely should get together one day and compare notes."

Smokey smiled sweetly. "Well, I'd better get back to my husband," she said, hoping to give Cantrell a clear message about her romantic status without offending him. For the first time that evening she was glad she had Hank as her "husband" and protector.

"How's it going with Handsome Hank?" asked Danielle, linking arms with Smokey as she stepped nervously away from the crowd milling around Vic Cantrell.

"Okay. Why didn't you tell me you were coming here?"

"I didn't know he was the one you were talking about. I really didn't know anything about him. He just said we were going to stop by a party."

"This is incredible. This may be my chance to get him to read my stuff."

"Sure. But I think you'd better pay more attention to your husband. Everyone else is." Danielle nodded toward the bar area.

There were swirls of people between them and the other side of the room, but Smokey could see Hank, a mildly amused expression on his face, surrounded by several eager women, including Milly Edwards.

"You know, I think it's the all-American good looks," said Danielle. "There's nothing fake about him. And he seems like a really nice guy. Maybe you should rescue him."

"He's a big boy," said Smokey. "He can take care of himself." But she started working her way across the room to where Hank stood. The women had mostly dispersed by the time she got there, and Mr. Girard had Hank by the arm, speaking intently, up close and personal, obviously about something important that he wanted Hank to hear above the noise of the crowd.

Paul Girard grinned broadly as Smokey approached. "This is quite a guy you've got here, Smokey," he said, patting Hank on the shoulder. "He's going to do some test shots for us."

"Test shots? I thought . . . What about the weight training?"

"Make a heck of a lot more money doing commercials," said Mr. Girard. "And Hank may just be what Fine Grains is looking for. Worth a try. No promises, but you wouldn't have to worry about tuition."

"What's he talking about?" said Smokey, as Paul Girard turned away to talk to someone else.

Hank was shaking his head and blushing. "Fine Grains is the cereal company that makes Elmo's Oatmeal, among other things."

"I know that."

"Seems they're looking to change their image. Want to do some commercials with a zing. Paul's words," Hank said apologetically. "The long and short of it is that he wants me to audition."

"Really."

Hank laughed. "Watch the attitude, *Mrs.* Bates."

"And what's this about tuition? Are you going back to school?"

"I've been in school for the past six years. Night school. Why do you think I'm so poor?"

"I don't know. I just figured weight lifters didn't make a lot of money. What are you studying?"

"I'm in my last year of law school. It's very all-consuming, but I'm beginning to see the light at the end of the tunnel."

"Law school? That's very impressive. But why didn't you tell me? What if it came up in a conversation with other people and I didn't know?"

"We were so busy talking about you, we never got to my deep, dark secrets," said Hank.

Danielle doesn't tell me she's dating Vic Cantrell, and Hank neglects to tell me he's in law school, and they're both the center of attention at my *party. I feel like I'm living a bad dream,* thought Smokey. She looked at Hank helplessly.

"Maybe we need to spend more time together. Get to know each other better." He draped his arm familiarly around her shoulders, and leaned forward to kiss her lightly.

Smokey's body went rigid, ready to push him away, but she caught a glimpse of people standing around them, smiling indulgently. *I've created a monster,* she thought. *And I have no choice but to play his game.*

Chapter Four

Hank slid the little Mustang smoothly into the parking space next to his ancient Subaru. "Nice car," he said, patting the steering wheel. "But you really should give Susie Subaru a chance."

"No thanks," said Smokey coolly. His car didn't seem so out of place now that she knew there was a reason for him to be driving an old clunker, but she still preferred to use her own car.

"So . . . it was an interesting evening," said Hank.

"It certainly was. And I'm certainly glad it's over."

"It wasn't that bad, was it? I thought we carried it off rather well."

"Yeah, you and Danielle were a big hit." Smokey's voice was tinged with sarcasm, but Hank chose to ignore it.

"We both made some good contacts. Even if I don't get a commercial, I met a couple of people who were thinking of hiring a trainer. And I think Danielle made a friend or two. I saw Paul Girard ogling Danielle, for one.''

''He was not! Paul Girard is a straight arrow. That's how I got this job.''

''We're all human, Smokey. And Danielle is very beautiful—although not my type. But I think there's more than that bothering you. Did something happen that I don't know about?'' Hank sounded genuinely concerned.

''No. I'm sorry if I'm irritable, but that whole scene—all those false pretenses—made me nervous. I just don't know how I'm going to maintain this sham marriage. I think I've dug myself into a big hole . . . that's going to get bigger—and deeper.''

''It's a job, Smokey. Your private life is your own business. I'll be happy to help you out any time you need an escort. Otherwise, just relax and enjoy the whole new world you'll be entering next week. You worked long and hard for this opportunity. Take advantage of it.''

''Thanks, Hank. I hope you're right.'' Smokey searched deeply into his incredible eyes. Maybe he wasn't so bad. At least he understood how serious her career was to her. Maybe he really would help her make it work.

''I am right,'' he said seriously. ''And I'm right about Girard looking at Danielle. There wasn't a man there who didn't look.''

Smokey punched him on the arm. ''Honestly! Is that all men think about? And just when I was beginning to think you had some redeeming qualities.''

Hank chuckled as he handed Smokey her keys. "May I come in for coffee? It's been so long since I've been out on the town, I don't really feel like calling it a night yet."

"Gee, I'd love to, but I think it's really too late for me," said Smokey, jumping from the car and heading for the apartment building. "Be sure and lock the driver's side door," she called back to him.

Headlights from an approaching car bathed her momentarily, then swerved to illuminate Hank as he stood beside the Mustang.

"Hank!" A female voice called out in the night.

Smokey turned and watched as Milly Edwards pulled her silver Honda Accord in beside the Mustang. Smokey stepped behind a bush and watched, hands on her hips.

"It's great having you for a neighbor," said Milly as she swooped out of her car. "I feel safe knowing there's someone I know in the parking lot."

"This is a great car," said Hank, walking around the exterior of the Honda. The conversation continued between Hank and Milly, but Smokey couldn't distinguish the words, only Milly's constant, high-pitched giggling.

Great, thought Smokey. *I forgot about my new neighbor on top of everything else that happened tonight. Surely Hank won't blow my cover.* Finally, she could stand it no longer. She had to know what they were talking about. She moved in closer.

"Smokey! I didn't know you were out here," said Milly, spotting her as she emerged from the shadows "Did you enjoy the party?"

"Yes, very nice."

"I was just telling Hank that he made quite a hit with Mr. Girard. He was still talking about him when I left."

"Really," said Smokey, smiling tightly.

"Listen, the night is still young," said Milly. "Would you two like to go somewhere and have a drink? I'd invite you to my place, but I haven't unpacked yet. Probably wouldn't be able to find a glass." Milly laughed as if she'd just told the world's funniest joke.

"Oh, I don't think . . ." said Smokey.

"Why don't you come up to our apartment?" said Hank, grinning mischievously. "We can make some coffee, can't we, honey?"

"Well, I . . ." Smokey was stammering.

"I can run down to the bakery for some pastries. . . ."

And leave me alone with this woman and this lie? I don't think so, thought Smokey.

"No, that's fine. Come on up," she said. She flashed Hank a warning look, but he ignored it and continued to chatter with Milly about her car.

"Oh, this is a mirror image of my apartment," said Milly when they opened the door. "And look, you can see straight across to it. It's the one right there. I left a light on."

"Isn't that something?" said Hank. "We can wave to you when we get up in the morning." He smiled warmly at Smokey over the top of Milly's head.

Smokey gritted her teeth and tried to force a smile

as Milly turned to her. "Why don't you start the coffee, Hank? Milly, sit down. Make yourself at home."

"You've really decorated this nicely," said Milly, looking around the room. Smokey had shopped secondhand stores for her furniture, so she was certain Milly was lying.

"Very feminine," Milly continued. "Not what I would picture for a man. . . ."

Alarms went off in Smokey's brain, but she managed to keep a tight smile plastered on her face. "Early marriage decor," she said. "Hank is rarely home. Between classes and work . . ."

Milly nodded sympathetically.

Smokey was seated in a chair facing the couch where Milly sat, and fortunately was the only one who could see Hank standing in the hallway, trying to figure out where the kitchen was hidden.

A smile of genuine mirth passed over her face as she watched him quietly opening doors, first to the bathroom, then a closet, before finding the entryway to the kitchen. Then she could hear him rubbing against the wall of the kitchen trying to find the light switch. *Serves him right,* she thought. *What was he thinking, inviting Milly to my home?*

Suddenly there was a crash as Hank tripped over something large. *Probably the trash can,* she thought. "Excuse me, Milly. Hank isn't very good in the kitchen. I'll be right back."

Hank was sitting on a chair, rubbing his shin, when she entered the room. "Hurt yourself?" Smokey asked, an evil grin on her face.

"I'm fine," he said indignantly. "Why did you leave that can in the middle of the room?"

"Tomorrow's trash day," said Smokey. "You should know that."

"Guess I missed that piece of information in your biography."

"Go on out and make nice with your guest." Smokey sighed. "I'll bring the coffee and some snacks."

By the time Smokey prepared a tray of cookies, poured the coffee, and returned to the living room, Milly had launched into her life story . . . and she was still only at kindergarten. Hank glanced up at Smokey in gratitude as she interrupted the tale long enough to serve the coffee. But the minute she sat down, Milly was off and running again.

She must be a very lonely person, thought Smokey as she sat listening to the high, whiny voice. *I wonder if that's what I'll be like in a few years. No one to talk to at home, so when you get an audience, you tend to be a little boring.*

She watched Hank and noticed that his eyelids were getting heavier and heavier. Every once in a while he would get up and move around the room as if trying to keep himself awake. *Good ploy,* she thought. *I wish I had thought of it, but it just won't do for both of us to be walking around, bumping into each other.*

Finally, Milly paused for a minute to take a breath and a sip of coffee, and Hank jumped to his feet.

"Sorry, ladies," he said. "I have an early morning study group. I'm going to have to hit the sack."

Smokey's mouth dropped open. *How dare you?* she asked silently, her eyes flaming at him.

"Oh, sure," said Milly indulgently. "I'll finish my story another time."

Smokey suddenly realized what Hank was doing, and she was tempted to get up and hug him for thinking of it.

"I just want to tell Smokey one little story about my sorority in college. It's girl talk, so you won't be missing a thing." Milly waved Hank off to the bedroom.

Smokey's face had a stricken look as Hank raised his hands in exasperation and hovered around the back hallway. He stood there for a few minutes, looking helpless.

Milly, following Smokey's stare, turned and saw him standing there. "Good night, Hank!" she called.

With an apologetic wave, he turned and entered the bedroom.

Smokey was extremely uncomfortable. She was dying to get into a nice, soft pair of pajamas, but she knew that as insensitive as Milly was, she would probably take it as an invitation to a slumber party.

And then there was the fact that she really was scheduled to work in the morning. She had given notice at the restaurant as soon as she was hired by Tri-Arts, but she had promised to work the early breakfast shift through the weekend since they couldn't find a replacement on such short notice. Smokey wasn't one to break her word, even though it was now well after midnight and she had to be on duty by 5:00 A.M. She stifled a yawn and smiled grimly at Milly, who hadn't missed a beat.

"Oh dear, look at the time," said Milly, glancing at her watch over an hour later. Smokey jumped at her words and realized she had actually drifted off for a bit.

"I'd better let you get to bed," said Milly with just a hint of annoyance in her voice. She must have noticed that Smokey's eyes were closed. "Maybe we can finish this tomorrow."

Smokey nodded, hoping Milly wouldn't take it as an invitation. "Why don't you go out through the sliding door?" she said, rushing to show Milly the way home. "It's faster, and I can watch to see that you get home safely."

"Oh, isn't this fun?" said Milly. "We can watch out for each other. I'll wave when I get my door open."

Smokey pulled the door closed and locked it as soon as Milly exited. Then she turned off the lights and pulled the drapes shut. "Wave away," she said, vowing never to open the drapes again.

"She's gone," Smokey called out, expecting Hank to jump out of the bedroom. She couldn't wait to light into him. She'd been saving up her wrath for a long time.

When he didn't appear, she called out his name. Nothing.

On tiptoes, she approached the bedroom door and peeked in. She heard the soft snoring before she saw him sprawled across the bed. He had taken off his jacket but otherwise was fully dressed.

"Hank," she said out loud, but he didn't stir. She kicked the side of the bed, but it didn't faze him. He was definitely down for the count.

I'll grab my pajamas and take a quick shower, she thought. *The noise ought to get him going.* She locked the bathroom door behind her and turned on the shower full blast. Fifteen minutes later, when she emerged from the steamy room, Hank was still dead to the world. It didn't look like he had moved a muscle.

In exasperation, Smokey grabbed a pillow, a blanket, and her alarm clock and stomped into the living room. *Since I have to be up in less than three hours, I guess it doesn't make much difference where I sleep,* she thought, fuming at the whole situation. In spite of her anger, she was almost instantly unconscious.

When the alarm rang in what seemed like only seconds later, Smokey had to think for a few seconds before she remembered why she was sleeping on the couch. Now she didn't want to wake the sleeping giant in her bed. All she wanted to do was sneak out of the apartment and deal with Hank Hudson, and his place in her life, later.

She entered the bedroom silently, and after checking that he was still asleep, she dashed into the bathroom to brush her teeth, wash her face, and pull her hair back into a loose ponytail. Then, just as she was slipping on her uniform in the closet, she heard him groan. She froze for a second, then stepped cautiously out into the room.

He had rolled over with his back to her. Smokey sighed with relief, and started moving toward the door and freedom. Just as her hand touched the doorknob, she hit her foot on the dresser and yelped in pain.

"What the . . . ?" Hank sat up and turned to look at her. His hair was all mussed up and he had the huge, puppy-dog eyes of a sleepy little boy.

"So, did you sleep well?" said Smokey, attempting to stay on the offensive in spite of the fact that she was jumping around on one leg as she grasped her throbbing toe.

"I guess I . . ."

"Fell asleep," said Smokey.

"Where did *you* sleep?" asked Hank, glancing at the other side of the bed.

"On the couch."

A slow grin passed over Hank's face. "Did Milly leave?"

"Yeah, but I told her to come back and talk to you first thing this morning."

Hank looked at her in alarm, then smiled again. "No you didn't. Where are you going?"

"To work. I've got the breakfast shift at the café. I'll be back around two. And you'll be . . ."

"Gone. I promise."

"Lock the door behind you."

"You could give me a key," Hank shouted to her back as she exited the room.

"Dream on," said Smokey as she slammed out of the apartment.

Smokey was dragging when she arrived home that afternoon. *I'm getting too old to survive on no sleep,* she thought, kicking off her shoes and sitting to rub her feet and examine her sore toe, a painful reminder of Hank Hudson and his role in her life. She looked around the apartment. The blanket and pillow were gone from where she had left them rumpled on the couch. When she went to the bedroom, the bed was made, and the room was neat and tidy.

She was standing, trying to decide whether to remove her clothes or dive directly into bed, when the phone rang.

"So what happened last night? Honestly," said Danielle's voice.

"What do you mean?"

"Hank answered the door when I stopped by this morning."

"Oh, great. What did he tell you?"

"That he fell asleep, and you slept on the couch."

"That's right."

"Oh, really."

"It wasn't like that, Danielle. He fell asleep waiting for Milly to leave. I couldn't wake him with a jackhammer. Besides . . ."

"Besides what?"

"I don't think he's really interested in me. This is strictly a business arrangement."

"Only if you insist on making it one. I think he's very interested in you."

"Why do you think that?" Smokey was definitely intrigued, in spite of her overwhelming fatigue.

"He was asking a lot of questions this morning."

"About what? And how long were you here?"

"Oh, I don't know. Hank made a pot of coffee. We talked."

"About what?"

"Well, he told me about Milly, for one thing. Said she was a crashing bore. And he was concerned about your having to work with her all day and then have her living right across the courtyard at night."

"He was concerned? Define concerned."

"Just a feeling I got. He wanted to talk about you, your job, all that. He asked why you weren't dating anyone."

"And you told him it was none of his business, I hope."

"No. I told him the truth. That you are committed to your writing. And honestly, Smokey, I admire you for that, in spite of all the grief I give you. I think Hank admires it, too, especially since he spends all his free time studying."

"So we're both nerds. Guess we do have a lot in common."

"I think it's kind of sweet."

"Well, right now I can't think about it. I'm going to bed."

Smokey was just starting to hang up when she heard Danielle screaming through the receiver. "Wait! Don't hang up!"

"What?" she said, putting the phone back to her ear.

"Hank said to tell you he left his home number on the kitchen counter . . . in case you have any problems with Milly and need him to come over."

"Fat chance," muttered Smokey, as she hung up the phone and flopped into bed.

Chapter Five

Milly met Smokey at the office door on Monday morning. "Mr. Girard is out of town for a week," she told her. "So I'm going to show you the ropes."

Smokey was hit with a sinking feeling. She understood that Milly's position in the organization was superior to hers, simply because of her close relationship with Paul Girard, but she wasn't looking forward to working for someone so bossy. Actually, Smokey had hoped for a low-key relationship with Milly at the office. It was kind of overwhelming to find out she was a close neighbor as well as a higher-up at work. She vaguely remembered Milly suggesting sometime in the wee Sunday morning hours that they carpool to work. Smokey had been uncomfortable at the thought, and she suspected that Milly had seen that in her face. Now they were in a position where Milly could boss her around and protect her superior position with Paul Girard.

It didn't help that Smokey hadn't gotten much sleep the night before. A filmstrip of the Saturday night party had persistently run through her head, and it always ended with a vision of Hank slumbering, sprawled on top of her bed, his dark eyes focusing on her when he woke up. Every time that vision appeared, she forced herself to think about how he had gotten all the attention at the party. It was supposed to be Smokey's new job, and hardly anyone had noticed her, while both Hank and Danielle had been the toast of the town.

But even that didn't bother her so much. It was her feelings for Hank that were all mixed up. In her more honest moments, she had to admit she was attracted to him, but she was angry that he hadn't been honest with her. Why hadn't he told her he was working toward a career in law? That he was more than a muscle-brained weight lifter? And why did she care? He was just playing a role. It meant nothing to him. Then why was he playing with her feelings?

Over and over in her mind Smokey had relived the party, the way Hank looked, the way she had treated him, refusing to ride in his car, not taking the time to get to know more about him. One minute she hoped he would call her, the next she didn't want to see him again. He had mentioned that he met with his study group on Sundays, but still, he could have called to thank her for taking him to the party. Most of the night she had paced, then tossed and turned, then paced some more.

She reminded herself that she had made a vow not to get involved with any man until, or unless, she had her career well under way, and then hopefully she wouldn't need a man anyway. And Hank obviously didn't have the time, or the means, to have a social life. So what was she stewing about? They weren't really involved—it was all just role-playing. Still, she hadn't been able stop her brain from churning, and now, on the first day of her wonderful new job, she was dragging from lack of sleep.

''These are the manuscripts Mr. Girard wants you to read,'' said Milly, pointing to a stack of paper over three feet high. ''You will write evaluations for him on the forms provided. But you probably won't have time to do that here. You can take them home with you. I'm short on office help today, so you'll have to help out.''

Smokey's lack of office skills became readily apparent within the first hour after she was put to work. Milly had set her up with an old electric typewriter in a tiny office with a small window looking out onto the reception area. She had a stack of contracts to type, and Milly would peek in every half-hour to check her progress. It was soon obvious that Milly was not satisfied with her output.

''I thought you said you could type,'' she said.

''I can,'' said Smokey defensively. ''You just didn't ask how fast,'' she murmured as Milly retreated, probably on her way to harass someone else.

Smokey's back ached and her mind was fuzzy when

the day finally ended at 5:00. She gathered up as many manuscripts as she could carry, and headed home, bone tired and discouraged.

"So much for the glamorous job." Smokey was stretched out on the couch surrounded by loose manuscript pages when Danielle stopped by that evening. "Where are you going?"

"It's a private showing of a new movie," said Danielle, checking herself in the full-length mirror. She was wearing a short, form-fitting red dress covered with red bangles, and she looked gorgeous. "It's not a biggie, but you never know who you might run into. Darren has just a small part but he told me to wear something that would get us noticed."

"Well, that ought to do it," said Smokey, smoothing the ragged terry cloth robe around her legs. "What about Vic Cantrell? Are you going to see him again?"

"Maybe. He's a little stuck on himself. Actually, a lot stuck on himself."

"He's a great writer."

"So he tells me. How about you? Heard from your husband?"

Smokey made a face. "No."

"Trouble in paradise?"

"Did you know he was in law school, Danielle?"

"Uh, yeah, I think he mentioned it. That's why he wanted to get some clients for personal training. So he could work better hours and earn money for tuition."

"Thanks for telling me."

"I thought you two had a meeting to learn everything about each other."

"We did."

"Well, I gotta go, Cinderella. Why don't you call Hank? Maybe we can all go out some night. Get better acquainted."

"Maybe. I've got a lot of work to do." Smokey pointed at the stack of papers beside the couch.

"You'd better strike while the iron's hot," said Danielle. "I saw how all those women were hanging on Hank the other night. You may find yourself in pretend divorce court."

Smokey stared at the door for a long time after Danielle left. She even reached for the phone once. Finally, with a sigh, she picked up another screenplay and started reading. "He could call me, you know," she said out loud.

The ringing of the phone jerked her out of a deep doze. Smokey sat up, totally disoriented. A glance at the wall clock told her it was only 9:00 P.M., but she had been asleep for over an hour. She stumbled to the small coffee table, grabbing the receiver just before the answering machine kicked in.

"Hullo?" Her voice was slurred from sleep.

"Smokey? Is that you?" Even though she had never talked to him on the phone, there was no doubting this was the deep, warm voice of her erstwhile husband Hank.

"Yes." Unconsciously, her voice changed to match his, low and slow.

"Did I wake you?"

"No. Of course not." Smokey was indignant.

"Oh, okay." There was a pause while Hank tried to gauge the direction this conversation was taking. "So how was your first day at work?"

"Fine. Okay. Actually, it was pretty miserable."
Smokey was shocked when the words fell out of her
mouth. Was she that hungry for a kind voice? Was
she already turning into one of those lonely old
women longing for an audience?

"Let me guess . . . Milly?"

His voice was so warm and understanding, the tears
Smokey had been repressing all day gushed in her
eyes and rolled down her cheeks. She gulped, trying
to stop the flow, but it just got worse, and before she
could say a word, the sobs were out of control.

Hank spoke softly and comfortingly, his words un-
important as they soothed her frazzled nerves. Within
a few minutes, she was able to get herself under control. "Sorry," she whispered. "I don't know what
happened to me."

"You needed to cry," said Hank. "Don't you feel
better now?"

"Yeah, I guess," said Smokey. "I had such high
expectations for the job. And Milly is squashing them.
I'm sure when Mr. Girard gets back, things will be
better. I just need to get through this first week." *But
what I really need is someone to hold me,* she couldn't
help thinking. *Especially a man who isn't frightened
off by a woman crying.*

"Has Milly been bothering you at home?" asked
Hank.

"No, but I keep the curtains closed."

"Smart move." Hank chuckled.

There was a moment of silence while they both tried
to decide where to go next with the conversation.

"Look, I'm sorry—"

"Thanks for cleaning—"

They both spoke at the same time, then stopped, laughing.

"Go ahead," said Smokey. "You first."

"I just wanted to tell you that I didn't intend to pass out on you Saturday night," said Hank. "I get so little sleep during the week, it's hard for me to keep my eyes open when I find myself in a prone position. You've got a great bed, by the way."

"Thanks," said Smokey, smiling in spite of herself. "And thanks for not leaving a mess for me to clean up."

"My mother trained me well."

"Good for Mom."

"Yeah, well, I just wanted to let you know that I've got final exams coming up in a couple of weeks, so I'm going to be hitting the books pretty hard. But if you need me for any social functions or anything, I could probably make some time. Just give me plenty of warning."

"I don't know of anything coming up, but . . ."

"But?"

Smokey swore she heard hope in his voice.

"I just thought maybe . . . you know . . . you'd like to come over. You could park your car in the lot for Milly to see. I could fix dinner, and we could talk."

"A real home-cooked meal? I'd kill for a good meal."

Maybe Mom didn't do such a good job after all. "Don't you cook?"

"I rent a room in an old house just off campus. I live on canned spaghetti warmed on a hot plate."

''I can do a little better than that. Want to set a time?'' Smokey hoped she wasn't sounding over-anxious, but she was genuinely—and surprisingly—excited about seeing him again.

''How about I call you, if I don't see you at the gym first. Either Saturday or Sunday. I'll need a break.''

''It's a deal! And Hank?''

''Hmm?''

''Thanks for listening.''

''Sure. No problem. I'll see you this weekend.''

Smokey hung up the phone and slid down the wall into a heap. Her heart was beating fast and her breathing was deep. *Now how am I going to get any work done? I'm not depressed anymore, and I'm certainly not sleepy. But how am I going to get this man off my mind?*

Smokey's typing was improving, but then it was bound to, since that was all she had done all week. Every day she begged for a computer/word processor so that she could work more efficiently, and every day Milly ignored her request.

By Friday, Smokey was having trouble talking herself into going to the office. She couldn't even work up the energy to dress smartly. Grabbing a flowered challis skirt and cotton knit top from her closet, she quickly threw herself together minutes before it was time to leave. *No need to dress like a stylish junior executive when you do the work of a back-room slave,* she thought.

She was bored out of her mind as she typed away

hour after hour. Through the small window she could see people coming and going through the outer office. Many she knew had to be clients, but she was never given the opportunity to meet any of them. She might as well be working in a factory, for all the experience she was getting.

Shortly after lunch, the door opened and Vic Cantrell walked in. He was accompanied by two men she recognized as top Tri-Arts agents. *Enough of this sitting here like a pheasant under glass,* she told herself. *I'm going to check out where the action is.*

Smokey didn't stop to turn off the humming typewriter, but jumped up quickly to get to the reception room while the three men were still standing there visiting. She heard a strange whirring noise behind her, but she was already at the door.

Vic was facing her little office, so he was the first to notice her movements. His welcoming smile was just a hint on his face when his eyebrows raised questioningly.

Smokey sensed something was wrong before she even saw the expression on his face. She had felt a tug as she reached the door but ignored it in her rush to the reception room. Now she could hear the whirring and clicking of the typewriter as she was suddenly stopped short. She looked down to see that the back hem of her long skirt was caught up in the typewriter. The flowered fabric sailed behind her to the desk, where she was snagged by the infernal machine, caught like some hapless animal.

Chapter Six

Smokey turned in time to watch in horror as a piece of her skirt disappeared into the laboring roller carriage of the electric typewriter. By now, she had the gaping attention of all three men as she stood frozen before them, watching their puzzlement turn to smirks of amusement.

At that exact moment the office door opened to admit Hank, looking very dapper in a stylish sports coat and pants. Within a matter of seconds he took in the scene, focusing on Smokey's expression of helpless horror. Without missing a beat, he hurried toward her, closing the door to her office and turning off the typewriter.

Minutes later, the men were gone, and Smokey sat sobbing in her small office as Hank worked with a screwdriver to dismantle the typewriter and disentangle the skirt's hem. Finally, he pulled the ink-and grease-stained fabric free.

"I hate this job," said Smokey, still sniffling. "I think I'm going to quit. I've made such a fool of myself."

"You're not going to quit," said Hank, taking her firmly by the shoulders as she finished smoothing the mangled hem of her skirt.

"Why do you care?" she asked bitterly.

"You're a very bright woman who has a lot to offer this company. And this is the best talent agency in town. The first week is always the worst. Just give it a chance."

"But that little scene just now. How can I forget that?"

"Worse things could have happened. Only a few people saw it, and if they can't forget it, they aren't worth knowing. You can't let a little thing like that destroy your career. If you quit now, you let them win."

"Them?"

"All those people in the world who don't want you to succeed because they know you're better than them. There's always going to be a 'them' out there. You just can't let them get you down."

Smokey looked at him with tears in her eyes. "I need a hug," she said.

Hank wrapped her in his arms and rocked her softly as he rubbed her back.

"You sound like a man who's had a bad week or two himself," she said.

"I've been fighting my own battles for a lot of

years. I've done a lot of things I hated doing, and a lot of people have put barriers in my way. But I'm going to reach my goal. I can see it up ahead now.''

"Law school?"

Hank nodded. ''I've had to struggle with crummy jobs, a failed marriage, people who said I couldn't do it—but next spring I'll graduate, and it will all be worth it.''

Smokey felt so warm and protected in his arms, she didn't ever want to let him go. ''Thank you for coming here today. You saved my life.''

"Actually, there is another reason I'm here," said Hank, checking his watch behind her back. "And I'm already late. I have an appointment with someone about doing a commercial.''

Smokey let go of him reluctantly. ''Fine Grains? The oatmeal deal?'' she asked.

"I think so. It's a big company that has a million subsidiaries. They just want to meet me. Tri-Arts is going to represent me if it works.''

"How exciting!" said Smokey. "You'd better get in there. Here, let me straighten your tie. Will you stop by and let me know how it goes?''

"Of course. I owe this all to you, you know. If you hadn't asked me to marry you, I'd still be lifting weights at the club.''

"You mean you quit your job?"

"No. Actually, I'm still lifting weights at the club. I was just trying to make you feel better.''

Smokey made a face and gave him a shove toward the door. ''Go on to your interview. And don't forget to stop by and give me all the details.''

"I won't," he promised. "You won't have to anchor yourself to a typewriter to get my attention next time."

Smokey sat hugging herself and smiling. Just a few minutes ago she wanted to crawl in a hole and never come out, but somehow he had turned the whole situation around and restored her self-confidence. How many men would have reacted to her predicament the way he did? Obviously not Vic Cantrell and his friends, who had stood and gawked at her embarrassment. Maybe she should reconsider her feelings about becoming involved with Hank Hudson.

Smokey typed on automatic pilot for the next hour or so, her eyes focused mostly on the lobby, waiting to catch a glimpse of Hank the minute he exited the inner sanctum. She had only turned her back for a few seconds when she heard a light tapping on the door frame.

"Are you decent?" asked Vic Cantrell, sticking his head around the corner.

"Funny," said Smokey, scowling.

"That was quite a little circus you put on," said Vic, entering the office and sprawling across a chair. "I'm just sorry it was so public."

"Yeah, me too," said Smokey, directing her attention to the typewriter. She was blushing furiously and she was angry at this man for making her feel that way.

"So how's your writing coming?" asked Vic after a few minutes of dead silence.

"Fine," said Smokey, looking up, surprised that he

had remembered. "I finished my latest last week. I'm letting it rest before I edit some more."

"Would you still like me to take a look at it?"

"Sure," said Smokey, reaching for her briefcase.

"No, I don't want it now," he said. "I've got an appointment with my accountant down the street and I don't want to drag it along. Why don't you meet me for a drink after work and we can talk about it?"

Smokey stared at the hundred-page manuscript she had pulled out of her briefcase. This was too big for him to carry? But then, maybe he really did need to talk about it first. She could give him some background, generate some interest to convince him he wanted to read it. "Okay, sure, where do you want to meet?"

"The Cosmopolitan Hotel? It's just down the street. They have a nice quiet bar. We can talk. Five-thirty?"

Smokey nodded. The last thing she wanted to do was go out in public the way she was feeling in her wrinkled skirt and tear-faded makeup, but if it meant getting her script read . . . After all, one word from a successful screenwriter and doors would open for her. Even those two insensitive jerks who had watched her struggle this afternoon would agree to read her screenplay if Vic Cantrell told them they should.

Another eternal hour ticked by second by second, before Smokey heard a commotion in the lobby and looked up to see Hank shaking hands with a group of people who were patting him on the back and smiling. After a few minutes of this, the crowd dispersed, and Hank walked to her office, grinning broadly.

"Good news?"

"You are looking at the new poster boy for Elmo's Oatmeal," said Hank, pirouetting clumsily into the office.

"Elmo's Oatmeal." Smokey giggled. "Somehow I don't see you as an oatmeal person."

"Oh no, I love oatmeal. Or at least, I will. I haven't eaten it since I was a kid, and the word 'yuck' comes to mind. But with the money they're going to pay me, I'll eat oatmeal six times a day, and love every minute of it."

"Big bucks? For oatmeal?"

"This is Hollywood, Smoke. Anything can happen. They want to give oatmeal a he-man image, and I'm going to be that he-man."

"Ah. The all-American boy grows up big and strong because he eats oatmeal."

"Something like that. At least Elmo's is going to pay my back rent and support me through finals and probably for a few months while I study for the bar exam. This couldn't happen at a better time. Ten years I've spent crawling through school, living on a shoe-string, scraping for tuition money, and now . . ."

"I'm really happy for you, Hank," said Smokey, standing to give him a hug. "You deserve this "

"Hey, I almost forgot. I took my car in for muffler work. Could I talk you into giving me a ride to the shop?"

Smokey started to open her mouth, but Hank jumped in.

"I know it's really out of the way, but there's a great restaurant nearby, and I feel like celebrating," said Hank, holding her tight. "I've got a few bucks left on my credit card, and I haven't been able to take a lady out to dinner for years. How about it? Just you and me?''

''Tonight? Oh, Hank, I can't tonight. I've got a meeting to go over my script.'' Smokey cursed herself for agreeing to meet Vic tonight. How she would love to spend a night on the town with this man who was getting more appealing by the minute.

''Oh. Well, that's good news. Who are you meeting with?''

''Vic Cantrell. He's agreed to read my stuff. I've just got to go.''

''Sure. Of course you do. We can celebrate another time. I'll use that credit card on cab fare.''

''Cab fare?'' Milly Edwards poked her head in the office door. ''Why do you need a cab?''

Smokey tightened her grip on Hank's arm, but he didn't get the clue.

''Car's in the shop,'' he said.

''Don't be silly! I can give you a lift. What are neighbors for?''

Smokey was amazed at the warm smile on the woman's face. Around the hired help, Milly was all business, but she was obviously blowing out all the stops for Tri-Arts's newest client. ''I need to have you sign some papers. Do you have time to come back to my office?''

''Yeah, sure,'' said Hank. ''In a minute . . .''

They watched as Milly walked through the lobby.

Hank shrugged. ''Consider this another assignment on our marriage contract. I'll catch a cab from your apartment building.''

"Go to Danielle's apartment. She'll give you a ride to the shop."

"Good idea. I'll need to talk to someone sane after a ride home with Milly."

"I'll probably be gone when you get through, but I'll—I'll see you later."

"You got it," said Hank, winking before he followed Milly to her lair.

Darn, thought Smokey, as she scurried around the little office putting things away. She felt unsettled by the events of the day. She should be excited about getting Vic's attention to her screenplay, but she couldn't erase the memory of his snide expression when she stood before him in her predicament with the typewriter. She didn't have a good feeling about him as a person, although she knew she should be grateful that someone as famous as Vic Cantrell would take the time to read her screenplay.

And then there was Hank. She tried to repress the warmth that spread through her when he was near, but there was no denying that he was awakening emotions that she thought were dead. And now she had to leave him trapped in Milly's clutches while she went to meet Vic, looking and feeling like someone who had been through a war.

Smokey spotted Vic sitting off in a dark corner of the bar. Something told her he was not on his first drink, and he didn't seem to have the energy to do more than half rise from his chair when she approached.

"Ah, the little office worker," said Vic, giving her

the condescending attitude she hated so much. "You didn't have to leave your beloved typewriter for me."

"Let's forget that little scene, okay?" said Smokey, carefully placing her briefcase on the vacant chair between them.

"Hard to forget, my dear. Hard to forget."

"Glass of ginger ale," said Smokey to the waitress who had suddenly appeared at the table. The girl gave Smokey a strained smile as Vic reached out to pat her arm.

"And bring me more of the same," said Vic, waving his hand over the empty glasses in front of him. With a grimace, the waitress leaned over to clear the table, giving Vic the opportunity to stare at her wolfishly.

Smokey was embarrassed for the girl, and also embarrassed for herself to be seen with this annoying man. She resolved to move the next empty glasses to her side of the table to spare this poor waitress any further grief. At the same time, she resolved to protect herself by keeping her distance.

"So, tell me how you got started writing screenplays," said Smokey, trying to divert Vic's attention back to the reason for their meeting.

Vic immediately launched into a detailed account of his favorite subject, himself, while Smokey struggled to act interested. An hour later, he was still talking and Smokey was on her third glass of ginger ale and listening to her stomach growl.

"I need to eat something," she said aloud, interrupting Vic's narrative.

"Talk to the waitress," said Vic, anxious to resume

the story that he obviously thought was fascinating her.

When the nachos arrived none too soon, the waitress presented a bill with them. "Sorry," she said. "The kitchen is a separate unit. I have to collect."

Vic looked off disinterestedly. "Do you mind getting it, Smokey?" he tossed out. "I'm a little low on cash."

Great, thought Smokey. *There goes my lunch money for the next week. For the next month, if I end up paying the bar tab too,* which was suddenly a very real possibility.

Smokey ordered a glass of water and quickly ate her way through the expensive plate of nachos. Vic was still talking, going into the minute details of his first sale, repeating word for word the negotiations between his agent and the studio that bought the screenplay.

The minute Smokey ate the last crumb on the plate, she sat waiting for Vic to take a breath. When he paused to empty his drink glass, she stood and pulled her screenplay from her briefcase.

"I didn't realize it was so late," she said. "I have lots of work to do for Tri-Arts." She gestured toward her briefcase and shook her head sadly. "I certainly hate to leave, but duty calls."

Vic looked at her cockeyed, his slack mouth hanging open.

"And speaking of promises, you made one to me. I'll just slip my screenplay in with your other papers here. Give me a call at the office when you finish reading it."

Without a backward glance, Smokey swept from the room.

What a waste, she thought. *It's not so much that he didn't ask for my screenplay, but that he turns out to be such an unpleasant person. And I wasted an evening I could have spent with Hank.* She felt even grungier than she had earlier and she couldn't wait to get home and change clothes.

There was a note from Hank taped to her door. *Help! Danielle has kidnapped me. Join us at the Shady Lady Restaurant?*

Smokey took a look in the mirror and sighed in disgust. It would take at least an hour to make herself presentable, and the note was dated two hours earlier. They had probably moved on by now, and she wasn't going to chase them all over town.

She couldn't remember ever being this tired and frustrated. In a fit of anger, she pulled off the offensive flowered skirt and threw it in the wastebasket. She tore up the note and threw it on top of the skirt. Then she put on her pajamas, grabbed the old, worn terry cloth robe, and headed for the couch, a stack of manuscripts in her arms.

A pounding in the distance penetrated Smokey's brain, but she couldn't move. There was a heavy weight on her chest, and, as she slowly regained consciousness, she wondered briefly if she was having a heart attack. She opened her eyes very slowly and looked down. She was still on the couch, covered with manuscripts. Smokey raised her heavy arm to look at her watch. It was 11:30 P.M., and the pounding was coming from her front door.

She slid the heavy papers on to the floor before cautiously approaching the door. "Who's there?" she asked hoarsely.

"It is I, the Oatmeal Man."

"And his loyal sidekick, Cereal Girl," chimed in Danielle's silly voice.

Smokey ran her fingers through her hair and adjusted her robe before opening the door. Hank and Danielle burst into her apartment.

"Surprise!" said Hank, grinning happily.

"Hank was afraid you might have company," said Danielle. "But I told him no chance." She laughed hysterically.

"Thanks," said Smokey dryly.

"We took a cab here because my car is still at the shop," said Hank with that same silly grin.

"We thought we'd help you rescue what's left of the evening. That stuck-up Vic Cantrell must have depressed you so much you wouldn't even join us," said Danielle.

"Wow, you guys are really something," said Smokey.

"Could you make us some coffee?" asked Hank. "I need to wake up enough to go home."

"I'll make coffee," said Smokey. "But I think you should get some sleep tonight. I know you've been studying awfully hard."

Hank stared at her with huge sad eyes for several seconds. "Maybe you're right. Let me go get cleaned up before the coffee. Smokey stood watching as he walked down the hall toward the bathroom, which was through the bedroom.

"Well," said Danielle brightly after Smokey had glared at her for a full minute. "You missed a good time."

"Obviously. But it's not my idea of fun to join a party already in progress. Especially when you are exhausted, sound asleep, and looking like you haven't washed your face in a week."

"Oh, phooey! Hank didn't even notice. And besides, this was his idea. He's been talking about you all night."

"He has?"

"Yep. And believe me, I tried to change the subject. But you can rest assured he's not interested in me." Danielle laughed as she sank onto the couch and pulled an afghan around her shoulders. "Are you going to fix that coffee?"

Smokey smiled and shook her head as she headed for the kitchen. So he had talked about her all night. She felt a warm buzz as she set up the coffeepot. She started to hum as she took mugs out of the cupboard. By the time she found a half-full bag of Oreo cookies and put them on a plate, she was dancing around the room.

In less than ten minutes she had a tray prepared and was carrying it out to the living room. But something was very wrong. The apartment was perfectly silent. Smokey placed the tray on the coffee table in front of the couch where Danielle was stretched out to full length, deeply asleep.

But where was Hank? Smokey stood at the half-open door of her bedroom listening for the sound of water running, anything to tell her there was a live body somewhere between there and the bathroom. Finally, she thought she could hear some breathing and she pushed open the door carefully.

The bathroom was dark, but Smokey could see Hank, crashed out yet again on her bed, snoring softly.

Smokey couldn't avert her gaze from his sleeping form. Hank looked so sweet, so innocent as he slumbered. But she couldn't help but notice the well-developed, muscular shoulders and chest tapering down to a narrow waist, undisguised by his polo shirt. His long, equally muscular legs protruded from khaki shorts. Smokey sighed in admiration. Hank had a slight smile on his handsome face and he seemed completely at home on the bed he had commandeered once again.

She stared at him for a long time, memorizing the scene, and then glanced furtively around the room, as if fearing that someone might have seen her. Regretfully, Smokey gathered the comforter that had been pushed to one side of the bed and gently covered her ''husband.''

She returned to the living room and sat on the floor in front of the coffee table. The coffee was getting cold, but she poured herself half a cup and grabbed a couple of cookies. *What do I do now?* she asked herself as she munched on the crunchy chocolate and savored the smooth cream.

Even though it was the weekend, Smokey had things to do and she needed to get some sleep. But where? The couch and the bed were the only two sleeping possibilities, other than the hard floor, and that simply wasn't an option. Smokey got up and went to the kitchen. She cleaned up the coffee mess and checked the cupboards for tomorrow's shopping list. Then she went back to the living room and gathered up the manuscripts from the floor. She was yawning furiously and she knew she wouldn't get any reading done.

Finally, she approached the bedroom again. Hank was just as she had left him, flopped on one side of the bed. Back in the living room, Danielle, too, was dead to the world. Smokey had no choice but to take her friend's apartment key out of her purse, gather up her nightgown, and robe, and go try to get some sleep in Danielle's apartment upstairs. Once there, Smokey made herself comfortable on the couch, relaxed, and in seconds was sound asleep.

Chapter Seven

The sun was shining through the window when Smokey opened her eyes again. But she couldn't see the window because staring at her were two pairs of eyes. Smokey screamed and jumped to her feet, pulling the afghan with her.

As she stood beside the couch looking at her two friends, shaking with laughter, the night before came rushing back.

"I forgot where I was," she said, gulping for air.

"I know the feeling," said Hank, sitting down and plumping pillows behind his back.

"You fell asleep on my bed. Danielle fell asleep on my couch. *I* needed a place to sleep."

"That's what they all say." Danielle was grinning. "Come downstairs to your place, Smokey. I'll make coffee."

"Oh, all right," said Smokey. She was pulling on

her robe, then pushed past Danielle and Hank on her way to the door.

Danielle looked at Hank and shrugged, then followed her friend downstairs. "So what's going on with you two?" she said, plopping in a chair in Smokey's kitchen and putting her feet up.

"Nothing," said Smokey tersely.

"Too bad."

Smokey gave Danielle a scathing look as Hank entered the kitchen.

"This was like a little slumber party, wasn't it?" said Danielle.

"Yeah," said Hank. "Guess we kind of crashed on you, Smokey. We appreciate the hospitality."

"Juice?" said Smokey, looking away.

"Sounds great. Have you got anything to eat?" Hank yawned and stretched his arms above his head. "I'm starved."

Smokey rolled her eyes at Danielle. "Let me check the fridge. Guess the Bates Motel is also turning into a restaurant."

"Here, let me look." Hank pushed Smokey gently toward the chair as he did a quick inventory of the refrigerator. "Ahh, good. Eggs, cheese . . . do you have an onion?"

Smokey pointed at a bowl on the counter.

"Great. Are you two up to one of Hank Hudson's world-famous omelets?"

"Wow, he cooks, too," said Danielle. "Smokey, you'd better nail this guy."

"I have a limited repertoire, but omelets are my specialty," said Hank. He was searching through the cupboards as he spoke. "Do you have an omelet pan?"

Smokey stood and went to help. The kitchen was small so she had to squeeze past Hank to get to the drawer where she kept her pans. Her heart was speeding as he leaned up against her, studying her collection.

"I'll take that one," he said, reaching around her to grab one of the pans in the back of the cupboard.

Smokey was paralyzed by his nearness, and at the same time strangely enjoying it.

"Hey, Danielle, do you know how to use a toaster?" asked Hank.

"Is that the little silver thing with the slots on top?" said Danielle.

"Thatta girl. You do the toast, and Smokey, you sit and watch. Because you were the hostess for this little soiree, we'll wait on you," said Hank.

Smokey grabbed a cup of coffee and did exactly as he said, her eyes following his every move as he dramatically whisked the eggs and grated the cheese. She couldn't remember the last time someone had cooked her a meal—probably back when she still lived at home in Iowa.

"Shouldn't we be having oatmeal?" said Danielle, searching through the refrigerator for butter.

"Hate oatmeal," said Hank. "But I may learn to love it if this deal works out." He grinned at Smokey as he flipped the smoking omelet over and slid it on a plate. With a flourish, he grabbed two slices of toast and presented his creation to Smokey.

"Gift of the gods," he said, standing beside her, waiting for her to take the first bite.

"Mmm, it really is good. You can come over to my house and cook any time."

"Invitation accepted," said Hank, beaming like a little kid who had built an intricate sand castle.

Smokey ate slowly while Hank prepared the next two omelets, and they all savored the feast together while Danielle entertained them with stories of her auditions for acting roles.

"But commercials can be very lucrative," she said. "Sometimes you have to do stupid things, like the time I was an eggplant, but you earn money every time they run on the air. If it's a good commercial, you can earn big bucks."

"I'm trying to picture you as an eggplant," said Hank.

"Not a pretty sight, let me tell you," said Danielle.

"Your big break is coming. I can feel it," said Smokey.

"You need to start digging through the trash cans at the agency," said Danielle.

Hank looked at them, puzzled.

"Remember? That's how I found out about the job opening for Smokey," said Danielle, and proceeded to tell him about the whole scene once again.

Somehow the story was even funnier when Danielle told it, acting out both her and Smokey's roles. They were all rocking with laughter by the time she finished.

"I'm not even going to ask how you picked me for the husband role," said Hank.

"I think it turned out to be a good choice all the

way around,'' said Smokey, openly admiring the man sitting at the table, rumpled and adorable. Her stomach was full, and her heart was warm as she sat surrounded by the two people who, she suddenly realized, she could count on to be her friends.

"Thanks. It certainly has worked out well for me," said Hank. His eyes sparkled as he gazed at her, setting her heart throbbing out of control. He finally broke the trance, blushing. Nervously, he checked his watch. "I've got a study group meeting in an hour. Need to clean up this mess and get going. I don't suppose I could use your shower?"

"Sure," said Smokey. "But I'll clean up the kitchen. You've done all the work so far."

"I insist." Hank quickly started grabbing dishes and running water in the sink. Within ten minutes the kitchen was spotless.

"He's very well trained," said Danielle as Hank left for the shower.

"Isn't he?" said Smokey. "This was a treat."

"Speaking of training, gym this afternoon? I'll pick you up at two. Got to sweat off all this partying."

"Sounds like a good idea," said Smokey as she saw her friend out the door.

The water was still running in the shower, so Smokey sneaked into the bedroom to grab a pair of jeans and a T-shirt. The water shut off just as she found what she was looking for, and she hurried out to the living room to get dressed.

She had just barely slipped the T-shirt over her head when the bedroom door opened.

"Well," he said, "you're dressed."

Smokey nodded, blushing, and hating herself for it.

"I wish I didn't have to go," he said, almost unconsciously speaking his thoughts out loud.

Smokey laughed. "I wish you didn't either."

"I could kick myself for sleeping through our 'date' last night," he said, moving across the room and gathering her into his arms. I'd like to spend more time with you," he said simply.

He smelled so fresh and clean and his strong arms felt just right. "Mmm, I'd like that, too," said Smokey, burying her face in his chest.

"Unfortunately, I've used up my free time for a while. In fact, I'm going to be playing catch-up all weekend. Paying for my little night out last night. A night out with the wrong woman." Hank sighed.

"So no dinner?"

"I can't." Hank gazed down at her. "You'd hate the life I lead," he said. "Between working full time and going to school full time, I have very little left to give anyone. But if you'll be patient, I'd like to try to get to know you better."

Smokey nodded. "Do you have to go?" She looked up at him with huge pleading eyes.

"Everyone in a study group has a responsibility to the others to show up and contribute. We've been together for three years, and we depend on each other. I can't let them down. But I'll call you later." He released her painstakingly, like he was attached with soft glue.

Slowly, his eyes reflecting sorrow and regret, Hank let go of Smokey's hand and grasped the doorknob to take his exit. Smokey leaned forward at the last minute for one final kiss, but jerked to a stop as, out of the corner of her eye, she caught movement on the other side of the partially open door. Hank, startled by the look of fear on her face, turned and yanked the door fully open.

"Milly! What are you doing here?"

"I live here," said the woman, in the same angry tone.

"I'm sorry," said Hank. "You just surprised me . . . us."

"Well, I was worried about you. I never saw your lights go on after I brought you home last night. I wanted to make sure everything was all right."

"Yeah, well, I went right to bed," said Hank. "Oh, no!" he said, looking at Smokey. "I forgot my car's still at the shop. I have no transportation."

"I'll give you a ride," said Smokey, grateful for an excuse to get rid of Milly. "I'm not doing anything until Danielle and I go to the gym."

"That would be great," said Hank, glancing at his watch. "Thanks, honey!" He leaned forward to give her a peck on the cheek.

Smokey hurried into the apartment to get her keys. Milly was still standing there when she returned. "Gotta go, Milly. See ya."

"Wait a second," said Milly, grabbing Smokey's arm while Hank hurried down the hallway. "I've been looking for a gym. Middle age is doing a number on me and I need to start working out." She patted her flabby stomach, and stared straight at Smokey.

How can you expect me to be your friend, the way you treat me at work? thought Smokey. *It's bad enough that I have to put up with your overbearing behavior there. Please go away.*

"So, what time are you girls going to the gym?"

"This afternoon." Smokey sighed with resignation.

"Well, why don't I just go home and gather up my things and come back. I'll just wait here until you're ready."

"No! Uh, I mean, we probably won't go until *late* afternoon. I'll call you."

"Okay," said Milly, giggling her irritating little-girl laugh. "This will be such fun. An afternoon at the gym with the girls. Maybe they'll give me a discount on a membership since I know Hank."

"No! You mustn't do that. They don't like it when employees ask for favors. They don't even know I'm Hank's wife." The alarm bell had gone off, and Smokey was babbling without thinking.

"Really?" said Milly in her somber, judgmental voice. "How odd."

Smokey's face was flushed as she stood helplessly in front of her nemesis.

"Well, whatever," said Milly. "I'll be waiting for your call." She wandered off down the hallway, humming to herself.

Smokey ran to catch up with Hank, her face horror-stricken.

"She's going to find me out," Smokey said on the phone to Danielle a while later. "I can't get rid of the woman, and now she's invited herself along to the gym. She'll brag about knowing Hank and find out he's not married. What am I going to do?"

"You can't make up some excuse?" said Danielle.

"She watches me like a hawk. And she'd determined to go to the gym with the 'girls.' "

"Well, then, we'll just keep her busy while she's there. We can give her the workout of her life. She won't have the energy to snoop."

"I can't imagine that happening."

Milly was carrying a little overnight bag that had to be twenty years old when they met in the parking lot later that day. Danielle looked at Smokey in amusement as they stuffed the suitcase in the car's trunk alongside their brightly colored duffel bags.

"I'm so excited," said Milly as they drove the familiar route to Vinny's Health Club. "I've always wanted to be part of the 'workout' group. And now, I've got you two to help me. You will help me, won't you?"

"Oh, yes," said Danielle. "We'll take you through our routines. You'll be an old pro in no time." She winked at Smokey.

Both women were further amused in the locker room a few minutes later when Milly appeared in her "exercise clothes." She waddled out of the restroom wearing an old swimming suit and a pair of black panty hose. "I'm ready when you are!" she sand out.

"Okay," said Smokey. "Let's get out to the stair-stepper."

Milly didn't even seem to notice the stares her outfit was getting from the fashionably dressed members of the club. In fact, she smiled and spoke to everyone she passed, telling one and all that it was her first time at the club.

"As if they didn't know," whispered Danielle in Smokey's ear. "Come on, Milly. Let me show you how to use the stair-stepper, and then we'll graduate to something harder."

Smokey got on the machine next to Milly and left the instruction to Danielle. But once Danielle had the older woman going and had hurried off somewhere, Smokey's concentration was interrupted by squeals of surprise and fear from Milly with each step she took.

"I'm going to fall!" yelled Milly, grasping at the air in Smokey's direction.

"No you won't," said Smokey firmly. "Just settle down and move like you are walking. Don't think. Just do it."

"This is so hard," said Milly a few minutes later. She was breathing heavily and her face was wet with perspiration. "I don't think I can keep going."

"Yes, you can," said Smokey encouragingly.

"Maybe there's another one that's easier," said Milly, letting the pads under her feet sink to the ground. "Let me try yours. It looks better."

"I've already set my timer. I don't want to stop until it buzzes," Smokey spoke firmly.

"Well, maybe I'll just wander around and see what else they have. Since you don't seem to be able to share."

Smokey exhaled a deep cleansing breath as the woman drifted off into the other room. "Why me?" she whispered. *And where has Danielle wandered off to? Probably off to join a different health club,* she thought.

Five minutes later, Danielle walked by and climbed on the stepper Milly had vacated. She said nothing, but she wore a mysterious smile.

"So?" said Smokey. "What are you up to?"

"Me? Nothing. I just got Milly set up with a trainer."

"Oh? And . . . ?"

"His name is Bruiser. He has a reputation for putting his clients through their paces. And he refuses to listen to whiners."

"Perfect," said Smokey. "This may be his biggest challenge."

"They deserve each other, don't you think?"

"Absolutely."

They found Milly an hour later in the locker room, bent over double, her face chalk white, trying to untie her sneakers. She looked up at Smokey and Danielle as they stood before her, her eyes pleading.

"Why didn't you warn me how hard this would be?" she asked. "My arms are too weak to pull my shoes off."

"Good workout, Milly?" asked Danielle as she bent down to help.

"That man should be arrested," she mumbled. "If I never see him again, it will be too soon."

"Maybe you should try a different trainer next time," said Smokey innocently.

"There won't be a next time," said Milly, struggling to her feet. "Take me home. And drive slowly."

Half an hour later, the two women had Milly deposited back at her apartment, a bottle of extra-strength pain reliever and a glass of water on the table beside her easy chair.

They were both silent until they reached Smokey's apartment and closed the door behind them. Then they exchanged high fives, and collapsed on the couch, laughing hysterically.

"There's a solution to every problem," said Danielle, when she was finally able to speak.

"What would I do without you?" said Smokey, gasping for air.

"Let's hope we never find out." said Danielle, giving her friend a hug. "We're in this thing together."

As expected, Smokey didn't hear from Milly for the rest of the weekend, but she also didn't hear from Hank. She floated through the days on the memory of his eyes gazing at her when she awoke, and the feel of his arms around her when he left. By Sunday night, she was pacing again, wondering why he hadn't called. Finally, at 8:00, the phone rang.

"Just got off work," he said. "Now I've got to study for a Contract Law exam next week. I just wanted to hear your voice."

"Why are you still working at the gym? Isn't Tri-Arts giving you an advance?"

"Not yet. Maybe this week. But I've learned not to depend on other people to do what they say."

"I know what you mean," said Smokey, thinking of Vic Cantrell.

"I'll talk to you later in the week. I'm supposed to

stop in and see Paul Girard. . . . Maybe we can have lunch.''

''Good. I have a feeling I'll need to see a friendly face,'' she said, thinking of Milly, and how miserable she was going to make Smokey's life in the week ahead.

Chapter Eight

Smokey approached the office the next morning with even more misgivings than the week before. But the minute she walked through the door, she sensed a different atmosphere than she had left on Friday. And the reason soon became obvious. Paul Girard was back.

The little office where Smokey had worked the week before was empty. Even the man-eating electric typewriter had been removed. It was as if the jail cell that confined her all week had never existed.

"Mr. Girard wants to see you right away," announced April, the receptionist.

Milly was frowning as she stood in the doorway of Paul's outer office. When she raised her arm to wave at Smokey, a flash of pain crossed her face, and Smokey struggled to look sympathetic. There was a noticeable limp in Milly's walk as she led Smokey through the inside door, and she groaned softly with each step. *That ought to keep you home in your rocking chair for a week or so,* thought Smokey wickedly. She knew all too well how an intensive workout could take its toll.

"Smokey," said Paul when he saw her approaching across the wide expanse of the room. Smokey breathed a deep sigh of relief when she saw the smile on his face.

"Well, we really hit the jackpot when we hired you. I think you're going to be an excellent editor," he said, patting the stack of screenplays she had evaluated and left on his desk. "And that husband of yours . . . the Elmo's Oatmeal people loved him. They're trying to create a new image, and they think Hank is the person to do it for them."

Smokey grinned and nodded. "You . . . you liked my evaluations?"

"Yes, you have very sensitive insights. I was a little surprised that you didn't get more done, but it was your first week, and things will get easier as you settle in."

Smokey could feel Milly's eyes boring into her back, but she resisted turning around.

"Do you like your office? I wanted you close so you could be here for last-minute conferences when I need you."

"The maintenance people were working in there all last week," said Milly, before Smokey could open her mouth. "So Smokey hasn't moved in yet. It's ready for her today."

"Where has she been working?"

"In that little alcove off the reception area."

"Oh. But you went over the company handbooks with her."

"You know how busy I've been, Mr. Girard. I'm afraid I didn't have a lot of time to spend with Smokey."

Smokey thought about the times over the past week when she'd seen Milly sitting around, joking with other secretaries in the office. And the two- and three-hour lunch breaks she had taken while Smokey was doing her typing and scut work.

Milly was smiling benevolently at Smokey, and Smokey smiled back tightly, and said nothing. Making an enemy out of Milly, especially in front of Mr. Girard, was not going to get her anywhere.

"Why don't you go ahead and get settled in your office, Smokey? We have a staff meeting this morning, and Hank's coming in this afternoon. So get to work and we'll see you in the conference room at eleven."

Smokey closed Mr. Girard's office door behind her and then stood there wondering where she was supposed to go. Paul had said her office was close, but where? She could go back in and ask Milly, and she was tempted to do just that, but she needed to wait a while longer before she confronted her. *When Paul Girard decides I'm indispensable, I'll take on the queen of mean,* she thought. *Until then, I'll play along with her.*

A few minutes later, Milly came out the door. She was still frowning and groaning as she looked at Smokey with raised eyebrows.

"My office," said Smokey. "Where is it?"

Milly pointed to a door on the other side of the hallway. "They'll be in to hook up the phone later this morning. You'll need to have everything arranged by then," she said, limping off to her desk.

The office was small but cozy. Bookshelves lined three of the four walls so there wasn't much decision-making to be done regarding where the desk would go. If the maintenance people had been working in there during the previous week, it was a mystery what they had been doing, since all of the furniture was piled in the middle of the room, surrounded by stacks and stacks of unread manuscripts. Smokey was going to have her hands full getting it settled in just a couple of hours.

By 11:00, Smokey had run her panty hose in three places, her dress was wrinkled, and she had streaks of dirt on her face, but she had everything arranged just as she liked it. She left notes for the telephone man and hurried to Paul's office for the meeting.

Milly had a major smirk on her face when she saw Smokey. Everyone in the meeting was dressed to the teeth. The male agents were wearing expensive Armani suits and the women wore ultra-chic power suits. Smokey glanced at the muted mirror that covered one wall and shuddered at what she saw.

"What happened to you?" asked Paul Girard.

"I was getting my office set up," said Smokey, glancing angrily at Milly.

"I thought the maintenance department took care of that," said Paul, searching for Milly, but he was interrupted by two of the agents who had a dilemma to discuss before the meeting began. "Why don't you take a second to go get cleaned up. I want to introduce you at the meeting.''

Feeling like a naughty little schoolgirl, Smokey did as she was told. The rest of the morning went by in a rush as Smokey sat fascinated through the staff meeting, listening to the high-powered agents discuss the big names and hot deals the agency was working on. It was fast-paced, exciting, and exactly what Smokey had expected the job to be. *Thank you, Hank, for encouraging me to hang on,* she thought.

The meeting lasted until well after noon, and then everyone seemed to disappear, off to power lunches and important meetings. No one invited her along, but Smokey was grateful to escape to her office, vowing to improve her wardrobe after the first payday. She was sitting on the floor, eating a candy bar she found in her purse, when there was a knock on the door.

''Come in,'' she said, thinking it was the custodian with another load of manuscripts for her to read. *Now I know why they filled this room with bookshelves,* she thought, stepping over the teetering stacks that had magically appeared while she was in the meeting. She pulled open the door and turned her back to it at the same time.

''Just find a space anywhere,'' she said.

''What is this? The book depository?'' said Hank, standing in the doorway, a McDonald's hamburger bag in his hand.

''Hank!'' said Smokey, obviously happy to see him. ''I think Milly is cleaning out the storeroom and sending it all up here. What's in that sack?''

"Hamburgers. I was betting that you wouldn't have had lunch yet."

"Good bet. Even if I had time, I'm not presentable enough to go out, even to McDonald's."

"Nice office," said Hank, looking around as he arranged paper-wrapped sandwiches and little sacks of french fries on the uncluttered desktop.

"Yeah. Seems Milly forgot to tell me I had one. It will be great when I get all this stuff put away." She bit into a juicy burger. "Umm, this is heaven." Smokey thought about her conversation with Danielle only a week or so ago when she said she wanted a man who could give her more than just McDonald's. With Hank it seemed like fun.

"Someday I'll be taking you to the trendiest restaurants for lunch," said Hank, as if reading her thoughts. "Of course you'll have to clean up your act a little bit." He looked pointedly at her raggedy panty hose.

"Someday I'll be a famous screenwriter and you can be my lawyer. We'll jet off to San Francisco for lunch."

"It's a date. I'm seriously thinking of specializing in movie law."

"Really? Getting the Hollywood bug?"

"This is pretty exciting stuff. And complex. I had one of my professors look at the sample contract Milly gave me. They get fifteen percent of everything I make. Get a few successful clients and it could be big money."

"Is that what you want out of law? Big bucks?"

"Not entirely, although that would certainly be a plus. I just find the movie business very interesting.

There wouldn't be a lot of boredom working in films, commercials.''

''Speaking of which, what time is your appointment with Paul?''

''In a few minutes,'' said Hank, glancing at his watch. ''Will you be there?''

''I haven't received my orders. He did mention that you were coming in today. Do you *want* me to be there?'' Smokey looked at him flirtatiously.

''When are we going to finish the talk we started yesterday?'' asked Hank, pulling her off the desktop and into his arms.

''Who feels like talking?'' said Smokey as their lips met.

''Who needs dessert?'' said Hank, coming up for air.

Smokey sighed contentedly and rested her head on his shoulder.

Suddenly a loud beeping sounded from the other side of Smokey's desk.

''What the heck is that?'' said Hank, irritated.

''My intercom. I think I need to adjust the volume.'' The buzzer sounded again, more insistently.

Smokey untangled herself and moved to push the button. ''Yes?'' she said.

''Smokey? Paul Girard. Have you heard from Hank?''

''Um, yes.''

There was silence on the other end. Then, ''Well, when is he coming in?''

''Actually, he's here right now, Mr. Girard. We were just having a bite of lunch.''

"Well, bring him in. Bring him in."

Smokey put down the phone and brushed nervously at her hair. "Now I look even worse than I did before," she said. "And I'm supposed to take you in to Mr. Girard's office."

"You look great," said Hank, taking her into his arms. "I love your hair when it's all messed up like that. Women who spray their hair like shellac make me crazy."

"Like Milly?"

"Like Milly."

Smokey let herself sink into his arms again. "I love the way you always make me feel good. You're always there to rescue me from myself. Thank you." She kissed him softly, then pulled away. "We've got to get in there."

The woman in Paul Girard's office was young and beautiful. She was dressed elegantly in an ivory silk suit, with a black silk blouse that framed her long, black, silky hair. Smokey ran her fingers through her tousled red curls and looked down at her wrinkled, dust-smeared skirt and suppressed the urge to hide in a corner.

"Hank, Smokey, I'd like you to meet Cherie Howe. Cherie is going to be your manager for this shoot, Hank. She will travel with you to the location and help make things easier for you."

Travel with him! thought Smokey in alarm. *He doesn't need her to travel with him. I'm available!* she wanted to shout. *I can "manage" him. I want to "manage" him.* She stepped forward to shake hands with Cherie, hoping her panic didn't show behind her plastered-on smile.

Smokey's mind raced as the three of them discussed the shooting schedule for the commercial. They would be leaving for the desert in two weeks, and would be on location for three days to a week, depending on how the shooting went. Smokey watched Hank's interaction with Cherie, searching for any sign that he was attracted to her. She was frowning when he turned and smiled at her, and she smiled hesitantly back.

The conversation drifted around Smokey for a while and then the office door opened and Milly entered, gingerly holding a sheaf of papers as she limped slowly across the room.

"Ah," said Paul. "Here's the important part. Your advance check. Half of what you will be paid. Minus our commission, of course. You can collect the rest at the end of the shooting. We need to go over the contract before you leave."

"Whew!" said Hank, staring at the piece of paper. "What am I doing in law school?"

"If this goes well, that will definitely be a question you'll want to ask yourself," said Paul, beaming at Hank.

An alarm sounded in Smokey's head. She didn't like the way things were going. Sure, she wanted Hank to be successful, but not at the cost of law school, and not with the help of Ms. Cherie Howe. *Money's not everything!* she wanted to scream. And then she remembered that money, or the lack of it, had been her objection to Hank in the first place. *Beware of what you wish for,* she told herself.

"So you can leave right after your last exam a week from Friday?" Paul was saying as Smokey's attention bounced back to the drama being played out in front of her.

Hank looked at her and shrugged. "Sure," he said.

"Cherie? Will you be ready to go?"

"Of course," said Cherie, smiling brightly at Hank. "The sooner the better."

Smokey put her hands behind her back to hide the fingernails she was digging into her palms.

When Hank went in to a meeting with the agency's lawyers, Smokey returned to her office. Suddenly, her enthusiasm for picking her way through the mess on the office floor had disappeared, and she sank down in a lump in the middle of the piles of manuscripts.

That was where Hank found her an hour later when he quietly slid her door open. Smokey was sound asleep in the middle of the mess, and she looked child-like and innocent propped up against the scattered papers, her head sunk against her chest.

Hank sat down beside her and kissed her gently on the lips. He sat back and watched as her eyes fluttered open. "Sleeping on the job?" he said, grinning.

"Oh, no!" said Smokey, jumping up. "What time is it?"

"Four o'clock," said Hank, checking his watch. "You've got another hour or so before you can legally sleep on your own time."

"I don't know. I think I'd better work late tonight," said Smokey, surveying the mess before her. "Especially since I've taken most of the afternoon off."

"Well, don't make it too late. I have plans."

"What plans?"

"First, I'm going to the bank." Hank waved the check in front of her eyes. "Then I'm going to the gym and resign my 'executive' position. And then, if you agree, I'll take you out for dinner."

Smokey glanced down at her wrinkled clothes. "I don't think you would want to be seen in public with me."

"You could change . . . or better yet, why don't you let me fix dinner for you? But you'd have to trust me with your keys."

"Sounds heavenly. But do you know how to cook? I mean, you do a wicked omelet, but can you do anything else?"

"You wait and see."

Smokey took her keys from her jacket pocket and handed them to Hank with a flourish. When Hank's hand enclosed hers, they both felt the bond that the passing of the keys signified.

"The timing on this whole thing is perfect. I have final exams next week, and now I'll have time to study for them and still spend tonight with you." Hank jangled the keys happily as he took his leave.

Smokey made like a tornado through her office for the next two hours. When she finally stood at the light switch surveying her work, she sighed with delight. The manuscripts were stored on shelves and the office seemed much bigger with a small couch, chair, and coffee table in one corner. *All I need are some green plants,* she told herself as she switched off the light. *I think I'm going to be very happy here.*

Chapter Nine

And I think I'm going to be very happy at home, Smokey told herself as she approached the door to her apartment. Delicious garlic smells were wafting out from under the door. Soft music was playing inside, and the lights were dim. A card table in the middle of the living room was covered with a white cloth and candles burned on either side of a lovely flower arrangement.

"How did you put this together so fast?" said Smokey as Hank appeared in the kitchen doorway, a full wineglass in his hand.

"Everything's easy when you have money. As opposed to when you don't, and you have to go pick the flowers yourself."

Smokey laughed as she pushed past him into the kitchen. "What are you cooking? It smells heavenly."

"Shrimp scampi, escarole and mandarin orange

salad, rice pilaf, and fresh bread. This is for you,'' he said, handing her the delicately fluted glass. ''Dinner's almost ready.''

''Thanks,'' said Smokey, staring up at him as she sipped the sparkling white wine. ''I think I'll go slip into something more comfortable.''

''I'll bet you use that line on all your husbands.''

''You've got my number already, don't you?''

''It didn't take long.'' Hank grinned down at her. ''Hurry along. There's nothing worse than overcooked shrimp.''

Smokey slipped into a skirt and a halter top, fluffed out her hopeless hair, and returned to the living room where Hank was waiting to serve her.

''Where did you learn to cook?''

''I've been on my own for a long time,'' said Hank. ''And one of my many jobs was in a restaurant. I was a prep cook, but I learned a lot just by watching the experts.''

''This is wonderful,'' said Smokey, tasting one of the juicy shrimp. ''I'm going to reek of garlic.''

''Join the club,'' said Hank, lifting a shrimp and saluting her.

Two bites later, there was a knock at the door. Hank and Smokey looked at each other. ''Danielle,'' they said in unison. ''Come in!'' yelled Smokey.

Danielle's face was flushed with excitement as she rushed into the room. ''I have news,'' she said. ''I just got a third call back on a part I auditioned for last week. It's a supporting role in their new vampire movie. But it's a *big* supporting role. And they want to see me again. Can you believe it?''

For a moment, Smokey was struck silent by the sight of her friend. Usually, Danielle was self-confident, her hard shell polished against attack, but tonight she looked soft, vulnerable.

"Of course I believe it. You have a lot of talent, and it's about time someone recognized it,'' said Smokey, getting up from the table to hug her friend as she jumped up and down.

"I didn't think I had a prayer after the first audition,'' said Danielle, "and then the second one went better, and now . . . I can't stand the suspense.''

"Sit down and join us,'' said Hank, pulling a chair over to the table. He left to find a plate in the kitchen while Danielle and Smokey danced around the room.

"I haven't eaten all day,'' said Danielle, finally taking a seat and stabbing a shrimp with her fork. "This is great— Oh wow, you guys were having a romantic dinner for two,'' she said, finally noticing the candles and tablecloth. "I'm sorry.''

"Don't be silly,'' said Smokey. "What are friends for?''

"To feed me and listen to me babble,'' said Danielle, blushing. "I'll be out of here in a minute. I promise. But this is soooo good.'' She poured herself a glass of wine and pulled the salad bowl toward her plate.

Smokey smiled at Hank as Danielle continued to chatter on. When the phone rang, she laughed as she rose to go answer it. A few minutes later, she was back.

"That was Milly," she said. "She isn't going into work tomorrow. Seems she's not feeling well." Smokey winked at Danielle. "She's got some papers that need to go into the office. She's running them over now. Well, actually, she's not running. It will be a while before she gets here."

Smokey and Danielle dissolved in laughter while Hank looked on, puzzled. When they finally managed to compose themselves again, they told him about their trip to the gym.

"You two are awful," said Hank, trying to look serious.

"I know," said Smokey. "But you have to admit that she brought it on herself. She insisted on coming to the gym, insisted on taking on too much. And she treated me like garbage all last week at the office."

"Yes, she asked for it," said Danielle. "If she wants to be one of the girls, she's going to have to develop some muscles."

"Besides," said Smokey, "it will give her something to think about, instead of snooping around here."

"She seems like such a lonely person. Too bad she doesn't have anything to fill her life," said Hank. "Except making other people miserable."

"Well, we'll be nice tonight," said Smokey. "Get another plate. And open another bottle of wine."

"Do you guys always eat in the living room?" said Milly a few minutes later when she was seated at the table, a glass of wine and a full plate in front of her.

"I think they were having a romantic dinner à deux," said Danielle.

"Oh," said Milly, clucking her tongue, the only part of her body that wasn't too sore to move. "You two act more like newlyweds than an old married couple. You know, that reminds me of a time when I was in high school and I invited this boy over for dinner . . . my parents were out of town for the weekend, and . . ."

"Here we go again," whispered Smokey to Hank as they carried their plates to the kitchen.

"I feel like I'm living in a girls' dorm," said Hank as he heard Milly and Danielle giggling in the other room. "Look, you go ahead and join them. I'll clean up in here and make some coffee."

"Thanks. I'll get rid of them as soon as I can." She ran her finger down his cheek and kissed him lightly on the lips.

An hour later, Hank was glaring from the couch while the three women continued to chatter. Every few minutes, Smokey glanced at him, and rolled her eyes. When Danielle finally took her leave an hour later, Milly stayed to go over the papers she had brought. It was another half-hour before she left, and then only when Smokey stood in the open doorway, arms folded across her chest.

Hank was yawning when Smokey finally fell into his arms, and soon they were both trying to keep their eyes open.

"I'd better get out of here," said Hank. "I've got an early class, and you have to be at work."

"Maybe tomorrow night?" murmured Smokey against his chest.

"I'm going to be up to my neck in studying from

now on. In fact, I should have been hitting the books tonight. I just couldn't pass up the opportunity to spend some time with you—alone.''

''I'm sorry. We should have gone out for dinner. My apartment seems to be Grand Central station lately.''

''You do have a lot of traffic through here. Look at me—I've already slept over two nights.''

''No big deal—it happens all the time.''

Hank looked at her closely.

''I'm kidding!'' said Smokey. ''Actually, you're the first male who's spent the night here, in *any* capacity. Honest. I'm a pretty boring person. I write alone every night.''

''I like boring. I'm looking forward to boring once I get through these finals.''

''And the commercial.''

''And the commercial.'' Hank sighed. ''Will you hang in there until this is all over? Till we can spend some time being boring together?''

''Of course. I'll look forward to it.''

The next two weeks were as grim as Hank promised. Occasionally, Hank would stop by for an hour or two, but he always had his books with him, and he would study while she wrote on the couch beside him. She did some of her best writing during this time. With Hank nearby, looking up and smiling warmly at her on occasion, she worked quietly and diligently at her computer, the words flowing effortlessly. If their world wasn't perfect, it was as close as they could get with the sword of law school hanging over their heads.

On the night before his last exam, Hank called to say his study group would be meeting far into the night, and he would be unable to get away, even for a few minutes. Smokey tried to hide her deep disappointment that she wouldn't get to see him again before he left. She tried to cheer herself with the reassurance that they would be together soon, but somehow she couldn't shake the premonition that things would never again be the same.

She paced the living room floor, unable to concentrate. But the walls of her small apartment echoed with his absence. They had been so much a part of each other for the last two weeks that Smokey ached with longing for his touch, his warm presence. Finally, she undressed, put on her old robe, and sat by the phone, willing it to ring, hoping beyond hope that something would change and he would be able to break away and come tell her good-bye in person.

She had just started to doze off when the insistent jangle of the phone jolted her to attention. *Hank,* she thought. It's got to be him. She grabbed the phone eagerly. "Hi," she sighed in a dreamy voice.

"Hi," said Danielle. "You okay? You sound sick."

"I'm okay," said Smokey, not even trying to hide her disappointment. "What do you want?"

"Want? I want to talk. But if you're going to be cranky . . ."

"Sorry, Danielle. Hank's leaving tomorrow, and I thought it was him calling. I just miss him so much, I'm kind of at loose ends."

"So big deal. He'll be back. A little separation might be good for your romance."

"I'd accept that, if it wasn't for Cherie."

"Who's Cherie?"

"She works for Tri-Arts. She's along as his manager. It's pretty obvious she can't wait to get him to herself."

"Hank seems like the ultimate one-woman man. I don't think you have anything to worry about."

"I hope not. I just wish he didn't have to study tonight."

"Sounds like you need something to take your mind off this guy. And, it just so happens, I have just the thing."

"What?" said Smokey listlessly.

"Party. Tomorrow night. The Sunset Roller Rink."

"Roller rink? As in skating?"

"Yep. It's great exercise, and lots of fun."

"What's the occasion?"

"I find out about the movie role tomorrow. They promised a decision by afternoon. We're going to party regardless."

"Oh, Danielle, I'm sorry. I've neglected you. You had your third audition and I didn't even call to see how it went."

"That's okay. I haven't been much fun to be around. I pace the floor night and day. But now I'm going to forget about it until tomorrow. Whatever happens, happens. I'm not going to worry about it anymore."

"Good for you. So who's going to be at your party?"

"Everyone I know. Vic Cantrell said he'd be there."

"Really. I have a hard time picturing him on a pair of skates."

"That's what makes this so much fun. Say you'll come."

"I wouldn't miss it." Smokey hung up the phone smiling. *Just what I need. Something to take my mind off missing Hank. Maybe a night out is just what I need to restore my writing schedule.*

One night of fun and games, and then it's back to the grindstone, she promised herself, never imagining in her highly creative mind the sharp left turn her life was about to take.

Chapter Ten

Hank was gone minutes after he finished his last final exam. He called from a pay phone outside the law library.

"Cherie's waiting in the car," he said. "So I can only talk a minute."

"Anxious, isn't she?" said Smokey dryly.

"Yeah. She's got the corporate jet waiting at the airport. She's very organized."

"I'll bet."

"I'm sorry we didn't have much time together. But at least my exams are over. And I have nearly a month before the next semester begins. We'll have a lot of time when I get back."

"I can't wait," said Smokey shyly.

"Me, either."

Smokey heard a car horn sounding in the background.

113

"I've got to go," said Hank. "I'll call you in a day or two."

"I'll be looking forward to it. . . . And Hank?"

"Yeah?" His voice was strained as the honking grew louder and more insistent.

"Take care . . . and be good."

"Always," said Hank. And then he was gone, and the receiver hung dead in her hands.

Smokey bought both knee pads and elbow pads on her way home from work that night. She was surprised at how much she was looking forward to the roller-skating party, an escape from her lonely, empty apartment. When Danielle called to tell her she had gotten the part, Smokey's anticipation for the evening soared. They were both in high spirits as they drove to the skating rink, turning up the music in the car and singing raucously all the way there.

"I think I'll rent a helmet," said Smokey, when she looked at the speed of the skaters at the rink. "I haven't been on skates since junior high."

"Yeah, me too," said Danielle. "All I need is a concussion after finally getting the job of my dreams."

Smokey found Vic Cantrell sitting at a rinkside table, his legs spread out in front of him. He had one skate on while the other foot wore only a sock.

"Are you going to skate like that?" she asked, taking the chair opposite him.

"It's the only way I can get around without falling flat on my face."

"You're not supposed to be walking around. You're supposed to be out there." She pointed to the rink.

"I was looking for the bar."

"I don't think there's a bar here," said Smokey. "This is kind of a kids' hangout."

"Shame," said Vic. "A bar would make it a much pleasanter place."

Smokey shook her head, but managed to smile tightly. "Haven't seen you around for a while."

"Finally got started on my next screenplay. I become very antisocial when I'm writing."

"But you came out tonight."

"Just finished the first draft. Needed a breather."

"I don't suppose you've had time to read my screenplay."

"Your screenplay? Did you give it to me?"

"Yes. That night at the Cosmopolitan Hotel bar." Smokey sighed as she watched the puzzled look on his face. "Just forget it. I'm going to try out my sea legs." She stood, angry and discouraged. She needed to move, work off her frustration.

"Hold it," said Vic, grabbing her arm. "I'll go with you. See if you can tie up this other skate, will you?"

Smokey was tempted to tell him to get lost, but, instead, she leaned over and grabbed his foot roughly, jerking the long shoestring as she lifted the skate to her lap.

"I love your style," said Vic as he leaned back on the bench and watched her avidly. "Are you always this assertive?" He raised his eyebrows questioningly.

"Yeah," said Smokey. "Now stand up and get out on the floor." She decided she wasn't going to be really happy until she could get rid of him.

Once on the floor, however, Vic grabbed her arm

in a death grip, and she knew if he was going down, she was going with him.

"Relax," she shouted over the loud rock music blaring from the speakers. The look of terror in his eyes made her laugh as she loosened his hold on her arm and took his hand in hers. "Bend your knees and take a deep breath."

By their second turn, Vic was starting to loosen up just a bit, but he had yet to move his feet. Instead, he coasted alongside Smokey, letting her guide him around the curves. After two circuits, he begged her to stop, but she refused, taking a perverse pleasure in her position of power.

"Hey, what are you two slowpokes doing?" Smokey first heard Danielle's voice coming from behind them, then watched in admiration as she slid in front of them, skating backward expertly as she carried on a relaxed conversation.

"You've been practicing," said Smokey. "Not fair."

"Had to have some way to while away the long evenings while I was waiting for the phone to ring. Come on, you two, speed it up a little."

Spurred on by the attention of two beautiful women, Vic finally moved his legs, and they picked up speed in their attempt to keep up with Danielle, who continued skating backward, taunting them to try to catch her.

"Look at me," cried Vic, shaking his hand loose and sliding his arm down Smokey's back.

"Let go!" cried Smokey, jerking away from his grasp. For just a fleeting moment she caught a glimpse of Danielle's horrified expression, and realized that Danielle could see what was going to happen before she did. Both she and Vic were so consumed with their personal wrestling match that they didn't realize they were flying out of control across the slate floor and hurtling at warp speed toward a gate that stood open in front of a sunken seating area.

Smokey was young enough and fit enough to react in a protective mode. She simply sat down, bringing her projectile movement to an abrupt halt. Vic, on the other hand, had not an athletic bone in his body, and his middle-aged physique had probably never seen a treadmill or a free weight. Physical activity, other than finger exercises on a typewriter, were unknown to him, and although he was aware of impending disaster, he had no clue how to react.

The next few seconds played out in slow motion as Smokey watched in horror. Vic, arms flaying, picked up speed like an airplane on takeoff as he flew toward the open gate. The world was silent for two ticks of the celestial clock, two ticks in which the music and voices and scraping of wheels against floor were strangely silenced. The crash, when it finally came, went on forever—wood splintering, broken glass tinkling, and a human scream piercing the air. All activity halted as Smokey and Danielle held each other's eyes in freeze frame.

Smokey perched by Vic's side in the ambulance on the eternal trip to the hospital. She had insisted that Danielle stay at the skating rink. It was, after all, her party. And Smokey was responsible for the "accident." Wasn't she?

It was after midnight when Danielle appeared in the waiting room, just in time for the doctor's grim report. Vic had suffered a concussion, a badly shattered left leg, and a fractured right arm. "Years of hard living and no exercise have taken their toll," said the orthopedic surgeon. "He will need private care when he leaves here. It will be a long, slow recovery. He's lucky to have friends like the two of you."

Smokey and Danielle looked at each other in alarm. Friends? They wanted to protest their innocence, but instead smiled sadly at the physician and listened to the details of Vic's treatment. "He's well sedated for the night," the doctor continued. "You might as well go on home. We can discuss the options for his home care next week."

"Home care?" said Smokey as she and Danielle trudged to the parking lot.

"He's got lots of money, doesn't he?"

"I guess." Somehow Smokey didn't think money was going to be the issue here. Responsibility, and a screenwriter with a broken writing arm, were going to be guilts she took home to bed with her. "Why did I ever agree to go out tonight? Sitting in my old bathrobe in front of the TV may not be very exciting, but at least it's safe."

The red light on her answering machine was blinking furiously when she entered the apartment.

"I guess you're not home," said Hank's voice plaintively. "It's Friday night and I'm sitting in a motel room missing you.'' He sighed. ''Guess I'll take Cherie up on her offer to buy dinner. I'll call you tomorrow.''

''Darn,'' said Smokey, wanting to kick the innocent machine.

But it was the next message that really made her want to crawl in bed and assume the fetal position.

''Smokey? Paul Girard here. I just got a call from Presbyterian Hospital. My name was on Vic Cantrell's insurance form as the person to call in case of emergency. They said you were with him when they brought him in but you didn't answer the page. I want to know what the heck is going on. Call me the minute you get in.''

The phone was ringing before the machine finished playing. ''What now?'' said Smokey, picking up the receiver.

''Smokey? I saw your lights go on.'' The accusation in Milly's voice made Smokey smile. She pictured the lonely woman standing at her door watching for the first sign of life in Smokey's apartment. *Yeah, so?* she thought, deciding not to comment. No point in encouraging her.

Milly ignored the silence for only a second. ''Mr. Girard is trying to get hold of you. You'd better call him right away.''

''Why don't you call him for me?'' said Smokey, sighing with exhaustion. There was no point in telling this story twice, and Milly would love feeling important.

Milly clucked her tongue. ''Well, I—I don't know what you did.''

"I didn't do anything. Mr. Cantrell fell at a roller-skating party. He suffered a concussion, broken leg, and arm, and he's resting peacefully."

Milly's sharp intake of breath spoke volumes. "Oh, dear," she said. "And what were you doing there? I thought Hank—"

"Is out of town filming the Fine Grains commercial. I was attending a party for a friend. Vic Cantrell was also a guest."

"Were you with him when he fell?"

Smokey hesitated, then decided not to offer any more information than necessary "I was close by, yes."

"How close?" asked Milly suspiciously.

"Mr. Cantrell had been drinking. He lost his balance," Smokey said tightly.

Milly sighed. "Well, I'll call Paul, but I'm certain he'll want a full report on Monday."

"I'm sure he will," said Smokey as she hung up the phone. She didn't even bother to wash her face before falling in bed, the phone tucked beside her in case Hank tried to call again.

Vic was in a lot of pain when Smokey arrived at the hospital the next afternoon. It was guilt as much as compassion that brought her there, as well as a hope that Vic would remember nothing of the circumstances surrounding his crashing descent into the skating rink pit.

"Smokey." He groaned. "What happened last night?"

"You fell down," she said dryly.

"Oh yeah," he said, looking pitiful. "Could you help me drink some water?"

A carafe sat next to the bed, so Smokey poured a small glass and held it to his parched lips.

"Tastes awful," muttered Vic. "What this hospital needs is a bar."

"Don't be ridiculous. That's what got you here in the first place."

"Not entirely, my dear. I seem to recall a certain ambitious young screenwriter giving me a healthy shove. A young screenwriter who wouldn't want that piece of information revealed."

"I didn't shove you. I was fighting off your unasked-for attentions. My husband would agree with my actions—in fact, he would definitely have something to say about all this."

"It's all academic, my dear. There's not much left here for your pretty-boy husband to take apart." Vic dramatically swept his one good arm across his broken body up to the leg hanging in traction. "The question is, who would your boss, the man whose income I pad, believe?"

Smokey squirmed in her chair as Vic stared her down.

"Now be a dear and get me my robe."

Smokey did as she was told, biting her tongue and clenching her jaw. "Now grab a pen and sit down. I've got a list of items I need from my apartment."

"I've got things I need to do, Vic. I can't spend the whole day—"

"But my dear, I'd be there to help you out if you

were strapped here in this bed. Especially if I were the cause of your distress.''

''How long are you going to be here?'' asked Smokey, ignoring his accusing words.

''Doc says a week, ten days, give or take. After the traction, there's therapy. Who knows?'' Vic took a long look at her.''

It was almost dark when Smokey got back to her apartment. She had made two trips to Vic's apartment. There were four messages on her machine, three of them from Vic and one from Danielle. Tears welled in her eyes as she dialed her friend's number.

''You're not his slave,'' said Danielle. ''No job's worth having to cater to Vic Cantrell's whims.''

''Easy for you to say, Miss Movie Star.'' She sighed. ''I don't know. We both got the job of our dreams, but mine came with a bogus husband, and a part-time nursing position. I'm living a lie, and now I have to add a guilt trip. It just doesn't seem fair.''

Smokey returned to the hospital reluctantly the next day to see if there was anything else she could do for Vic.

''Well, there are those delicious little tea sandwiches they have at that Turkish restaurant off Rodeo Drive,'' he said. ''The food here is abominable.''

Smokey shook her head in disgust and turned to exit the room. ''Forget it,'' she whispered to herself. Head down, she didn't notice the door to the private room swinging open as she approached, and she was knocked backward by the impact.

"Whoa," said Paul Girard, grabbing Smokey to stop her from falling, and at the same time dropping a huge bouquet of flowers from his arms. "Are you okay?"

"Yeah, sure," said Smokey, still off balance. "Mr. Girard! Nice to see you." She glanced nervously back at Vic, who was still glaring at her. Now she was dead. Girard's timing couldn't be worse. She gathered up the flowers and followed Paul Girard to Vic's bedside.

"Gee, Cantrell. You must have taken quite a spill," said Paul, examining Vic's mummified body. "How did this happen?"

In the silence that followed, Smokey shifted her weight from foot to foot, staring at Vic with pleading eyes. Finally, Paul turned to her for an answer.

"He fell," she said simply. "I guess he was going too fast." She smiled weakly. "Look, I've got to go pick up some things for Vic. I'll be back in an hour. Give you two a chance to visit."

"Sure, sure. You go ahead." Paul threw his arm around her shoulders as he walked her to the door. "This is great that you're looking after Vic. Got to get our client back on his feet, you know." He eyed her meaningfully.

Smokey could see Vic over Paul's shoulder, grinning slyly.

Smokey had a sick feeling in the pit of her stomach as she pulled out of the parking lot and headed for her apartment. *I think I must have lost my mind to be shopping for him like this,* she thought. *Besides, I've got to check the answering machine.*

But there were no messages. Why hadn't he called?

She wanted to kick herself for driving all the way
home just to check a sleeping answering machine. She
would have to drive to the restaurant and back to the
hospital. It would be late when she got home and she
would once again fall into bed without writing a word.

Life was certainly more simple before I got this job,
she thought. *I never dreamed I'd long for the good
old days of waitressing at the Wayside Café, and writing screenplays at night, but from this perspective they
don't look so bad.*

"They said the first one went really well," said Hank,
calling from a small motel near Las Vegas a few days
later. "I find that hard to believe. I mean, it took almost a week to shoot a thirty-second commercial! Fine
Grains just gave us the go-ahead to shoot a second
one. We'll be moving to another location tomorrow. I
don't know when I'll be back."

Smokey tried to swallow her disappointment. Every
muscle and nerve in her body ached for him. Hearing
his voice just made it more unbearable.

"How's Cherie?"

"She's great. I couldn't do it without her help."

"I'll bet."

"Gotta go. We're packing up. I'll call you as soon
as I can."

Vic called the next morning and asked that she come
in to meet with his doctor, and Paul Girard gave her
a few hours off "to represent the firm." Smokey
didn't like the sound of it, but Paul had added Vic's

care and maintenance to her job description, and she had become the designated gofer.

''Mr. Cantrell will be ready to go home in a week to ten days,'' said the doctor without preamble. ''He tells me his apartment is on the third floor of a building with no elevator. He's going to be in a wheelchair, so this is an impossible situation. Any ideas?''

All eyes were on Smokey as she fidgeted under the gaze of Vic and his doctor. ''A nursing home?'' she said hopefully.

''No openings for at least two months. By that time, Mr. Cantrell will be fairly mobile.'' The doctor continued to watch her.

''Didn't you mention you had a first-floor apartment? Poolside?'' said Vic.

''A pool would be excellent therapy,'' said the doctor.

''But my apartment is very small. And I'm at work all day. I don't think . . .''

''You'd only need room for a hospital bed. There would be a nurse during the day.''

''But my husband . . .''

''I thought Paul said Hank was on the road filming commercials,'' said Vic. Was that a sneer on his face?

''Yes, but not forever. . . .''

''It will only be for a few weeks,'' said the doctor. ''The home nursing crew will take care of most of his needs. You won't even notice that he's there. But he needs to have someone around if he finds himself in trouble during the night.''

Like if he gets thirsty, thought Smokey. The idea of coming home from work for a little relaxation and solitude and finding the obnoxious Vic Cantrell waiting for her truly repelled Smokey, but she had a feeling she wasn't going to win this battle. She suspected Paul Girard knew all about it when he had waved her out of the office earlier that morning.

"I'll think about it," she said. "Right now I need to get back to work." The atmosphere in the room was suffocating her and she couldn't wait to get some fresh air.

Smokey left the hospital, knowing in her heart that the decision had already been made, even though she hadn't agreed to anything. *Some people get away with murder on a daily basis, but I shove one guy's hand away, and I end up taking care of him for the rest of my life.*

She longed to have someone to share her misery. Where was Hank when she needed him?

Chapter Eleven

Danielle had started work on her movie and was rarely home. The shooting schedule was grueling, she told Smokey that weekend, but she was loving every minute of it.

"And then, there's Nick," she said, barely controlling the excitement in her voice.

"Nick?"

"He plays opposite me. Not the lead, but a substantial role. And he's so good! He's being touted as one of Hollywood's up-and-coming talents. And he's soooo cute." Danielle swooned like a love-struck teenager. "I think I'm really in love . . . for the first time."

"When do I get to meet him?"

"Why don't we plan something? When does Hank get back?"

"Soon, I hope. He finished the second commercial

and he and Cherie flew to Michigan to tour the Fine Grains offices. Meet the company executives and all that.''

''Wow! Doesn't that make you jealous—him spending all that time with that Cherie chick?''

''No,'' Smokey said too quickly. ''Well, actually yes, but there's not much I can do about it.'' She was suddenly overcome with the waves of unhappiness she'd been trying to suppress since Hank left.

''It'll be okay,'' said Danielle. ''He's crazy about you. I can tell.''

''You haven't seen Cherie. She's gorgeous.'' Just saying the words made Smokey more miserable. ''But Hank promised he'd be home by next Sunday. The first commercial is going to run that night, and he swore he'd be here to watch it with me.''

''Oooh. A premiere! Kind of. Why don't we get together for that?''

''That's a great idea. Bring Nick over and we'll make an evening of it. Come early . . . for dinner. The commercial airs halfway through the 'Sunday Night Movie.' ''

''Prime time, huh? We'll be there with bells on.''

By three o'clock Sunday afternoon, Smokey was beginning to despair over whether Hank was going to make it. She had prepared a huge pot of spaghetti sauce, and was putting the finishing touches on the salad and garlic bread. Earlier in the day she had vacuumed and rearranged the TV viewing area and set the VCR. Now she had nothing else to keep her mind off the tardy guest of honor.

And then, all of a sudden, there he was. He had come straight from the airport and was carrying a garment bag over his shoulder. Deeply tanned, he stood in the middle of the living room dressed in khaki shorts and a dark green polo shirt and looking gorgeous.

"I had the limo bring me here. I didn't want to waste time stopping at home and cranking up Susie Subaru," he said, taking her into his arms.

And suddenly, everything seemed all right. All the worrying, all the jealousy over Cherie, all the abuse from Vic, vanished with those few words. Hank was home and he was anxious to see her.

"I've missed you so much," they both said in unison. Then, embarrassed, they both stopped and laughed.

"I worry about you spending so much time with Cherie," said Smokey, the words out before she could stop them. "She's so . . . well, glamorous, and she gets to spend more time with you than I do."

"Cherie means nothing to me. She's a great manager, but that's it. Even when we were being wined and dined by the corporate executives, I couldn't think of anything but getting home to you."

"Now I know you're putting me on. You'd rather be here eating spaghetti than dining in style with the beautiful people?"

"That's what I like about you, Smokey. You're so down to earth. You're a good friend to Danielle and even Milly. You have a mind and you're not afraid to use it. You don't need all the fancy stuff. You're just comfortable with yourself. There aren't many women like that out there.''

"Well, thanks . . . I guess," said Smokey.

"I really do mean it in the best way. I mean, you have a natural beauty, but there's more to you than that. I couldn't stand being with one of those women who is destroyed by a broken fingernail. Oh, I know I'm not saying this right. I just wanted to tell you how much I missed you. How anxious I was to get home and hold you in my arms. I think you're going to be a very important part of my life, Smokey Bates.''

"Ah, that's what I wanted to hear," said Smokey, snuggling up close to the man she had dreamed about every night he was gone. "I want to be a very important part of your life.''

"Good."

They snuggled on the couch, content just to be together once again.

"Your stomach's growling," said Smokey, finally coming up for air.

"I'm starving. And that spaghetti smells so good. Maybe I should sample the sauce?''

"Just a small taste," said Smokey, following him out to the kitchen.

"So what's this Nick like? Another one of Danielle's oddball dates?''

"I have no idea. I haven't met him. But Danielle's crazy about him. I've never seen her this smitten.''

"Really? I can't imagine anyone taming that wildcat.''

*   *   *

Danielle and Nick were set to arrive at 6:00 P.M. so they could have dinner before the big moment. At precisely 6:00, there was a knock on the door.

"I like him already," said Smokey. "This is the first time I can remember Danielle being on time for anything."

Hank went to answer the door, and Smokey heard loud voices and wild laughter. She hurried out from the kitchen to find a gorgeous man in a tuxedo accompanied by Danielle in an evening gown topped with dazzling jewels including, but not limited to, a sparkling tiara.

"The invitation said premiere," said Danielle haughtily.

"What invitation?" said Smokey, giving her friend a hug.

"Hank, Smokey, I'd like you to meet Nick Larson, the new vampire in my life."

"Glad to meet you, Nick. Danielle needed a new vampire. The old one was getting a little long in the tooth," Smokey joked.

Nick was one of those people who looked at home in a tuxedo, and yet his face was open and friendly and his eyes sparkled with a natural sense of humor and enjoyment of life. *At last,* thought Smokey, *Danielle's found a normal guy.*

After a short time, Nick and Danielle had both darted into the bedroom and returned in shorts and T-shirts. "The joys of having a whole wardrobe department at your disposal," said Danielle. "We couldn't resist."

"And may it be the first of many premieres for all

of us,'' said Smokey, clinking her wineglass against Danielle's.

The dinner conversation was lively and hilarious, and they barely finished in time to gather in front of the television for the unveiling of the first commercial at 8:20 P.M. Smokey switched on the VCR just minutes before it began.

The scene was a western desert diner where many he-man, blue-collar types gathered for breakfast. The hairy, unshaven, macho men sat at the bar with scowls on their faces and ordered steak and eggs, bacon and hash browns. Then in walked Hank, sleeveless T-shirt exposing his magnificent muscles, his face cleanly shaven, definitely blue collar, but definitely all-American boy. He was shown in a full-body shot walking his graceful athletic walk. When he sat at the bar, the waitresses were peering out from their stations all over the diner, and his hard-boiled waitress fanned herself before stepping out of the kitchen to wait on him. Even then, she could hardly speak, she was so taken with him.

"What can I get you?" she asked, chewing hard on a wad of gum.

"Oatmeal," he said.

"Oatmeal," she said.

The next scene showed Hank eating his bowl of oatmeal, while flirtatious waitresses hovered about. Several women in booths were also dipping into bowls of oatmeal. The hairy types were looking even more disgruntled. Finally, one pushed his plate of steak and eggs away and, pointing to Hank's bowl, said, "Bring me one of those . . . with a side of hash browns."

The screen went blank and the words FINE GRAINS. WINNING AMERICA'S HEARTS appeared.

Smokey, Danielle, and Nick started to cheer the minute the commercial ended, and Hank stood and took a bow.

"Hokey," said Danielle, "but also very attractive in a weird way."

"*Very* attractive," said Smokey. "I just can't believe you got paid all that money for saying one word."

"It's all in the delivery," said Hank. "You've got to know how to project."

They watched the commercial over and over several times, before adjourning to the kitchen for coffee and dessert. When the phone rang, Smokey picked it up on the second ring.

"Did you watch the commercial?" Paul Girard's voice bellowed in her ear.

"Of course," said Smokey.

"Let me talk to Hank."

Smokey handed the phone to Hank. She rejoined the conversation with Danielle and Nick, but kept an eye on Hank as he conducted an extended conversation on the phone. He wore a guilty smile when he rejoined the conversation at the kitchen table.

"What did he want?" she asked.

"Paul? Oh, he had heard from the Fine Grains people. They were pleased. He just wanted me to know."

"That was nice of him," said Smokey, but she had a strange feeling about the call. Hank was thoughtful for the rest of the evening, his jovial mood somewhat tempered. Danielle and Nick seemed to sense this and they left for home shortly thereafter.

"Okay, what's up?" said Smokey as they were cleaning up the kitchen.

"What do you mean?" said Hank.

"You got quiet after Paul called. What did he say to you?"

"Nothing." Hank went out to the living room to gather up stray glasses. "Well, actually, there is something," he said when he returned.

"Okay. Give."

"The Fine Grains people want me to go on a cross-country publicity tour. You know, promoting the product. I'd be gone for several weeks. I don't know . . ."

"The new semester starts soon. You can't do it." Smokey turned back to the sink where the dishes were soaking.

"The thing is, they're really pushing for this, and . . ."

Smokey turned back to look at him.

"Well, they're offering a lot of money. I could finish school and set up my own practice with the money they're dangling. . . ."

"Oh." Money again. But then, she had to remember that Hank had been going without for a long time. And how many times had she said that she was only interested in a man with a real career?

"When would you leave?"

"Two days."

"Oh." Smokey could think of nothing else to say. She had such great hopes that they would have this time together, to get to know each other better. And then a thought occurred. "Will Cherie be going with you?"

"Of course. I told you, she's a great manager. I don't know what I'd do without her. All I have to do is show up. She does all the work."

"That's great," said Smokey without enthusiasm. "You're lucky to have her."

"That's for sure."

You are so clueless, thought Smokey. *All men are. Well, Ms. Cherie Howe, maybe Hank thinks you're harmless, but I know better. And I'm going to give you a run for your money.* "So, we've got two days. Let's make the most of them." She slipped into Hank's arms.

Hank held her in his warm embrace before pushing her gently away. "Can we save this for tomorrow night? I'm beat, and I need to go home and unpack, and repack. Let's plan a big evening tomorrow. The sky's the limit."

Smokey was disappointed, but for the first time, she noticed the dark circles under Hank's eyes, the exhaustion lining his face.

"Okay, but I'm not going to let you off the hook this time. I want a real celebration. Just the two of us."

"I promise," said Hank, kissing her deeply and leaving her leaning weakly against the door when he left.

Everyone in the office was excited about Hank's performance the next day, and by the end of the day, the ratings were coming in and it was obvious that this was going to be a prize-winning commercial . . . and Hank was going to be a star.

"Can you believe all this fuss over an oatmeal commercial?" said Smokey to Danielle when she called the office to gossip about Nick and the night before. "They're calling Hank the hottest thing in advertising."

"Ah, advertising, the Shakespeare of the nineties," said Danielle. "None of my commercials have been as successful as his, but I've made enough money to support myself. What does that say about us as consumers?"

"It says we're a gullible bunch of people. Oatmeal sales are picking up. Fine Grains loves Hank."

"I'll bet. It's not easy to sell oatmeal. Ugh."

" 'Entertainment Tonight' is going to interview him next week, and they've gotten some feelers from the 'Late Show' in New York."

"You're kidding. For saying one word? You'd better hang on to that guy. This may all go to his head."

"I don't think so. Not Hank."

She hoped she sounded more confident than she felt.

Smokey's world came crashing in later that afternoon with a call from Vic's doctor. "We're ready to release him. I've ordered his supplies sent over to your apartment this afternoon."

"You mean he'll be at my place tonight? I have plans . . . I'm not ready. . . ."

"We can wait until tomorrow, if that will be more convenient."

Hank will be gone tomorrow, thought Smokey. *But*

what am I going to do when he comes back? Everyone thinks we're married. How am I going to explain why he stays in his own apartment? And what am I going to do with an invalid in my apartment? Especially one as obnoxious as Vic Cantrell. I'll never get any writing done. I'll never have any privacy. How did I get myself into this mess?

I've got to think on the bright side, she told herself. At least Vic wouldn't be released until after Hank was long gone. And, she would have someone to keep her from getting desperately lonely without him. If it were just somebody she liked . . . anyone but Vic Cantrell.

She was still giving herself a pep talk when the phone on her desk rang again. For a moment, she considered not answering it, as if that would make all her problems go away, but on the fourth ring she picked up.

"I have good news and bad news," said Hank, without greeting.

"The good news first. Please," said Smokey.

"I'm doing Letterman next week. Cherie's a whiz at setting up these things. Can you believe it?"

"Hardly. What's the bad news?"

"We have to leave tonight. Cherie has filled the calendar with interviews. We have to be in Chicago tomorrow morning."

"I knew it," mumbled Smokey.

"What?"

"That Cherie, she's something else, isn't she?"

"I told you she was a good manager."

"Yes, you did. She does know how to manage people.'' *Right out of my clutches.* ''So, will I get a chance to see you before you leave?''

''No. Cherie's coming by in a few minutes to go over the schedule, and then we're heading for the airport. I'm sorry. Will you take a rain check on that night out?''

''Of course. I just wish . . .''

''Me, too. But my public calls . . .''

''Yeah, right. Your public, and Cherie Howe.''

''Look, someone's at my door. Probably Cherie herself. I'll call you later.'' He was gone before she could say another word.

Just as well, she thought, *because I have a feeling I would have said something I would live to regret.* Depressed, she dragged through the rest of the day, and left work as early as humanly possible without calling attention to herself

As it turned out, Smokey didn't have a lot of time to think about Hank's schedule, or even his absence. When she arrived home from work, dragging a load of scripts and trying to keep her chin from rubbing on the ground, she found two men at her door visiting with Danielle.

''What's going on?'' asked Danielle. ''I know I haven't been around much, but why do you need a hospital bed? You could have called.''

''I don't need a hospital bed. In fact, it's the last thing I need. Who sent you guys?''

One of the burly men pulled a slip of paper from his shirt pocket. ''A Dr. Peasley at Presbyterian Hospital. Yep, this is the right address.''

Smokey sighed deeply. "Okay. Give me a few minutes to rearrange the furniture. Help me, Danielle?"

Puzzled, Danielle followed her into the apartment. "Presbyterian Hospital? Does this have anything to do with Vic Cantrell?"

"It has everything to do with Vic Cantrell. My new roommate."

"Lucky you," said Danielle. "Whatever happened to your pretend roommate, the Oatmeal Man?" She grabbed the end of the couch and helped Smokey drag it to the far corner of the room.

"He's on the road, selling America's favorite breakfast gruel, thank goodness," said Smokey as she stacked the coffee table on top of the couch. "I only have room for one man at a time in here."

Half an hour later the living room looked like a garage sale, with the massive bed in the center and all the furniture stacked around the edges.

"Don't think you'll be winning any awards from *House Beautiful*," said Danielle, surveying the scene.

"I think it's hot-fudge sundae time," said Smokey, surveying the damage while shaking her head. "I need to get out of here."

"Wait till you have that sorry lump of humanity in that bed." Danielle shuddered. "Ice Cream Palace here we come. My treat."

Chapter Twelve

Smokey was called home from work the next morning to take delivery of one ill-tempered Vic Cantrell.

"Take the rest of the day off," said Paul Girard. "You'll need to get him settled in."

"I'll be back in an hour," said Smokey tightly. "He has a day nurse. My shift doesn't start until evening."

The ambulance arrived seconds after Smokey pulled into the parking lot. The chubby little nurse who accompanied her patient already looked strained as she pushed the wheelchair into the building.

"There's a bump up ahead," snarled Vic as the nurse pushed the chair up a slight incline. "I'd hate to have you miss one."

"Be nice," said Smokey, smiling at the embattled nurse. "If she quits I'm going to send you to a home for the terminally crabby. And they aren't going to take any guff from you there."

"Get me a drink," said Vic once they had him settled in bed, and the nurse was in the kitchen getting herself a glass of water.

Smokey did as she was told, and presented him with a bill from the liquor store which had made a delivery the night before. "A check will be fine," she said. "And they won't be back until I receive payment."

Vic scowled.

"I've got to get back to work," she called out to the nurse. "Have a wonderful day."

She drove back to the office slowly, wondering how she was going to survive the next few weeks. Vic irritated her every time she was around him, and her mood wasn't that congenial to start with. The office, even with Milly making life miserable, never seemed so inviting.

"You're going to have to find a replacement for Nurse Nancy," Vic growled the minute the day nurse was out the door that evening. "She's dumb as a board. All she does is sit and watch soap operas, for heaven's sake."

"I'd be more than happy to see if Nurse Ratchet is available," said Smokey.

She was standing by his bed trying to figure out what to do with herself. Between the bed and Vic's wheelchair there was no place to sit except a small patch of carpet. "Let me get you settled and I'll go back in my room and do my work."

"Please. I can't stand to watch another minute of inane television. I need some adult conversation."

He looked so pitiful that Smokey couldn't refuse.

And for the first time, maybe in his life, Vic Cantrell made an effort to be pleasant. He asked Smokey about herself, about her writing, about her future. He admitted that he hadn't read Smokey's screenplay yet but he promised to do so while he was staying at her apartment.

Smokey still didn't trust him, but she sensed that he was at least making an effort, and she decided to relax and let go of her anger. She was surprised to find herself laughing at one of Vic's hospital stories when there was a knock at the door.

"Probably Danielle," said Smokey, steering the wheelchair over to the door. "Checking to see if we've killed each other yet."

The smile on her face disappeared when she pulled the door open. "Milly," she said. "What a surprise."

"You never leave your drapes open." Milly pushed her way past the wheelchair. "I didn't know if Mr. Cantrell had arrived safely."

"Safe and warm," said Vic. "Join us?"

Smokey graciously surrendered the wheelchair to Milly Edwards, and hurried to the kitchen to grab some ice, grateful to find a means of escape. By the time she returned, Milly had launched into one of her long, boring stories, and Vic was staring at her with glazed eyes.

"Hold on there a minute, woman," he said as Smokey refilled his glass and offered a fresh one to Milly. "Don't you ever shut up?"

Smokey ducked her head in shock, waiting for the fireworks to begin. No one talked that way to Milly Edwards. No one. But to her surprise, there were no fireworks. Instead she heard Milly's deep, throaty laugh. Minutes later, both Milly and Vic were totally unaware of Smokey's presence as they carried on a ranting conversation, interrupting each other, each trying to get the upper hand in the exchange, and neither one succeeding . . . or failing.

"I'm going to my room. Need to rinse out some things," said Smokey, but neither Vic nor Milly was paying any attention. Grabbing a quick sandwich in the kitchen, Smokey settled on the bed with her laptop computer and lost herself in a world of words, brought back to reality only occasionally by raised voices and laughter from the living room.

It was almost midnight when Milly peeked in the bedroom door to tell her she was leaving. "He's all tucked in for the night," she said. "I don't know when I've had so much fun." Giggling softly, she left quietly.

"The world's two most boring people," said Smokey to Danielle a few days later when they met at the gym. "Why didn't I think of getting them together sooner?"

"I've always said there's someone for everyone," said Danielle. "So, does she come over every night?"

"Like clockwork. And the beauty of the whole thing is that she's too talked out to cause any trouble at work. Just a little bonus for us all."

"And what do you hear from the Oatmeal Man?"

"He calls. But he's usually in a hurry to get somewhere. He's leaving for New York this weekend. Scheduled for the 'Late Show' on Wednesday."

"No kidding? that's the big time. Why don't you

come over and watch it with Nick and me? Come for dinner. Give the lovebirds an evening alone.''

''You've got a deal. Besides, I wouldn't be able to hear a word of the program with the nonstop discussion going on in my living room.''

''David Letterman will kill him,'' said Nick when they gathered in front of the television to watch the program. ''He could make him look ridiculous.''

''Hank called when they finished taping. He said he thought it went well,'' said Smokey. But still, she was biting her fingernails for him.

''I hope they get his marital status correct,'' said Danielle, looking at Smokey meaningfully.

She was referring to the ''Entertainment Tonight'' segment that had run earlier in the week portraying Hank as the gorgeous new ''hunk.'' Although they didn't say Hank was single, they hinted that he was available, although possibly involved with someone unknown.

When Smokey asked Hank about that comment, he said they had never asked him if he was married, and he suspected the agency had glossed that over in order to make him more appealing.

''Would you have said you were married if they had asked?'' she said.

''Of course. I'm not going to blow your cover, Smokey. A deal is a deal.'' Hank sounded irritated.

That wasn't exactly what she wanted to hear, but she excused his attitude to the insane schedule they were running him through.

Finally, the ''Late Show'' came on the air, and

Smokey sat impatiently as Dave interviewed another guest, a gorgeous woman who was a star in a new television sitcom.

''Did you get a chance to meet Hank Hudson backstage before you came on?'' Dave asked at one point in the interview.

Smokey sat up, suddenly at full attention.

''Yes, I did,'' said the starlet. ''He could certainly make me convert to oatmeal.''

The audience laughed and Dave proceeded to tell them that Hank would be out in a few minutes to show them how to make the perfect bowl of oatmeal.

''A cooking segment? He didn't tell me he was doing a cooking segment.'' Smokey looked at Danielle in horror.

''Have you got the VCR turned on, Nick? This should be worth saving.''

Finally, the commercial was over and Dave introduced Hank. The women in the audience screamed as he strolled on the stage, looking gorgeous in jeans, an opened-neck shirt, and sports coat. The applause went on and on as he stood with Dave for over a minute. Hank was grinning self-confidently and his eyes sparkled as the camera focused on his face scanning the appreciative audience.

He and Dave talked briefly about the commercial and how successful it was. Dave kept referring to Hank as the ''new sex symbol.''

Smokey hardly took a breath as she watched her boyfriend/husband, now more a stranger, a public possession, chatting comfortably on national television. *He's mine!* she wanted to shout. *He's my husband*. But the truth of the matter was that he wasn't, and they both knew it.

They went to another commercial, promising to come back and cook oatmeal.

"He's doing great," said Danielle. "He has a real knack for putting on the charm. He'll make a great lawyer."

Smokey hadn't told her friend about her fears that Hank wouldn't make it back in time for the next semester. And now, she couldn't help but wonder if Hank was reconsidering his career choice. He had become a real celebrity, and she could be losing him to his new life.

Her fears were increased when the "Late Show" returned. A small kitchen was set up and both Hank and Dave were wearing aprons while two gorgeous female models hovered behind them. Things quickly got totally out of hand as the two men started fooling around with the oatmeal, throwing gobs of it at the audience. Then Dave got out the whipped cream and soon they were all covered with the sticky stuff. The audience, including Danielle, was roaring with laughter as they cut to another commercial break.

"That was great," said Danielle, rolling on the floor. "You didn't think it was funny?"

Smokey was sitting stony-faced in her chair. "Yeah," she said, forcing a smile. "It was real cute." *But it would have been a lot cuter if it were someone else's boyfriend*, she thought. The idea of Hank having so much fun with those two models, and on national TV to boot, was really bothering her.

* * *

Hank didn't call again until the next night. He sounded tired and didn't talk long, promising he would be back in a week or so, and they could talk then.

"Get a baby-sitter for your live-in invalid," said Hank, reading her mind. "Or better yet, get rid of him. We're going to go out on the town." *Easier said than done,* thought Smokey. Milly as a baby-sitter would be no problem, but she resented the fact that she and Hank couldn't enjoy the privacy of her apartment. They needed time alone, time to get to know each other better, time for Hank to convince her that he wasn't getting caught up in his new lifestyle.

Chapter Thirteen

Smokey was staring into space in her office one morning the next week when the buzzer on her intercom sounded. She was dreaming about Hank and his promise to be home that weekend. She had specifically told the office staff that she was going to read manuscripts and didn't want to be disturbed, so she was irritated that someone was ignoring her request.

"Yes," she barked into the speaker.

"Smokey?" Paul Girard's voice blasted forth.

"Yes." Smokey struggled to erase the irritability from her voice.

"Can you come in here for a minute." It was a statement, not a request.

"Sure." The last thing she wanted today was to spend time listening to Paul ramble on for the minute that he always turned into an hour or two. And, as always, he would have more work for her. Everything

148

with Paul was an emergency, and she often ended up working after hours finishing up a script evaluation or preparing a report that he wouldn't get around to looking at for days. Sighing, she grabbed a legal pad and headed for his office.

Paul was seated at his desk, reading a manuscript that Smokey immediately recognized as her screenplay. After a minute he looked up and smiled at her.

"Vic Cantrell sent this over by messenger a day or two ago. Said I needed to look it over."

Crusty old Vic had come through for her after all? Smokey had all she could do to keep from standing and shouting. "And what do you think of it?"

"I like it," he said.

"You do?" Now she wanted to dance on his desk.

"Yes. I think it's got some real possibilities. I've made some suggestions in the margins." He held up a sheet of the typed paper, almost completely covered with handwritten notes. "If you want to work on this over the weekend, I have a meeting with Tom Rogers at Astonia Studios on Monday, and I'll take this along and make a pitch for it. But I'll have to have it on my desk first thing Monday morning."

"Sure," said Smokey, taking the stack of paper from Paul Girard's outstretched hand. "First thing Monday morning."

Smokey waited until she'd closed the door to her office before she did her dance. Jumping up and down and hugging herself, she finally picked up the phone and called Danielle to share her news.

"It's going to take me all weekend to fix this," she said, leafing through the pages. "All weekend with no sleep.'' Every page was covered with notes. This was going to be a very major project.

''I'll deliver food and good cheer every four hours,'' said Danielle. ''You've got to get it perfect.''

''I know. Tom Rogers! Can you believe it? He's the biggest producer in the business.''

''Too bad about Hank. But maybe he'll be too tired to notice.''

''Uh-oh. I forgot about Hank. I mean, that's all I've been thinking about . . . until five minutes ago.''

Smokey had dreamed of nothing else but the feel of his arms around her ever since she learned he was finally coming home. How could she have forgotten so quickly? And what was she going to do about him?

After all the flattery and attention, beautiful women, and exciting places Hank had experienced over the past few weeks, Smokey knew she was going to have to give him a very special homecoming if she wanted to keep his attention. And now, here she was with the most important project of her career, just at the time she needed to entice him back into her life if she wanted to keep him. If he was even interested anymore.

Maybe if I work all night tonight, she thought. *But even at that, it's going to take the whole weekend. Surely he'll understand.* Smokey was pacing by now, trying to sort out her life and develop a plan.

Let's see, she thought. *I've got a boorish, demanding man with a hospital bed and a wheelchair in my living room. And he's got a lazy nurse during the day, and a shrill, overbearing friend at night. I've got a gorgeous boyfriend expected home after several gruel-*

ing weeks on the road, surrounded by beautiful women, and anticipating a passionate welcome from me. And I've got the project of my life, my very future demanding every minute of my time between now and Monday morning. Just a typical working girl's problem, that has to have a very simple solution. Right?

Wrong, an inner voice answered. *But I've got to start somewhere,* she told herself, as she left her office and walked purposefully down the hallway to Milly's office.

She was sitting at her desk, a dreamy look on her face, and she jumped when Smokey approached her. Milly was dressed in a simple cotton dress that was well cut and flattering to her figure. Or had she lost weight? Even her hair, usually overstyled, was framing her face in an expertly styled pageboy style. Her face was glowing and Smokey couldn't help but think that Milly looked ten years younger than she had when Smokey first met her. Once Milly focused on Smokey, she grinned broadly, causing her face to look even younger.

''What's up?'' she said.

''I've got a problem, Milly. Actually, I've got a bunch of problems.'' Smokey proceeded to spill her whole story on Milly's lap.

''Vic will be delighted to hear about your screenplay,'' said Milly dreamily when Smokey had finished her tale of woe.

Maybe I've got the wrong office, thought Smokey. *This isn't really Milly Edwards, Dragon Lady of the Tri-Arts Talent Agency.*

''Well, I can solve part of your problem,'' said

Milly, grinning once again. "We'll just move Vic over to my place. We've been talking about doing that anyway. We just didn't want to hurt your feelings."

"Hurt my feelings?" Smokey was sputtering, but Milly didn't seem to notice.

"I'll be over after work. We can move Vic in the wheelchair. The bed shouldn't be any problem if we take it through the sliding doors."

"I'll call Danielle to come help. Thanks, Milly." Smokey rushed out of the office, stopping to take a deep breath as she leaned against the closed door.

A song about the scarcity of rain in Southern California kept running through Smokey's mind as she stood staring out her patio doors waiting for Milly and Danielle to arrive and start the great moving project. The perpetually sunny skies were covered with swirling clouds, and big splats of rain hit the cement walkway outside.

Vic's nurse had gathered her things and left without a word when Smokey arrived. Her days were surely torture, but she was the most humorless person Smokey had ever met.

"Did you tell Nurse Nancy that you were moving?" said Smokey, stepping back into the living room where Vic sat huddled in his wheelchair.

"No. We don't talk. Milly can call her tonight." Vic's mood was more surly than usual, which was usually the case in the late afternoon, before his soul-mate arrived.

"Did Milly tell you about my screenplay?"

Vic grunted.

"I really appreciate your help, Vic. You know, sending it to Paul and all. I . . . well . . . thank you."

Vic grunted again, and Smokey smiled. *It was probably the first nice thing you've ever done for anyone,* she thought, *but I'm not going to grovel. You owe me, you old coot.* Once again, she glanced at her watch. *And I can't wait to get you out of my hair so I can start to have a life.*

Milly and Danielle arrived minutes apart but Milly wasted little time with the other two women as she hovered over Vic, refilling his glass and fussing over him. She pushed the wheelchair to the patio doors and stood studying the weather.

"It's not raining now," she called to Smokey and Danielle. "I'm going to take him on over."

"Does Vic know what he's getting into?" asked Danielle as they witnessed the two of them rolling around the edge of the swimming pool, Milly talking a mile a minute while Vic waved his hands animatedly.

"Don't know, don't care," said Smokey. "At least he's out of my life and he seems happier. Let's move that bed before he comes to his senses."

Nurse Nancy's duties didn't include housekeeping, a fact that became abundantly clear when they pushed the bed from its moorings. Books, newspapers, towels, and dust bunnies littered the floor under and around the bed.

"Yuck," said Danielle.

"Let's just get it out of here. I've got work to do." Smokey was biting back tears of frustration.

Getting rid of Vic was just going to be one step in

her return to normalcy, whatever that was. Smokey had long forgotten. The dust balls that drifted around the room as they pushed the bed toward the sliding doors might require a professional cleaning service. When was she ever going to find the time to make things right?

Smokey and Danielle pushed the heavy wheeled bed through the door and out onto the cement without a glance at the weather. At the near edge of the pool they stopped to take a breath and at the same moment the skies opened up and hurricane-force gusts of wind drove the pelting rain down.

There was no escape for the two women as they struggled to keep the bed moving on a straight line away from the edge of the pool and out of the lapping waters beckoning to them.

"This is the first time I didn't think Milly's apartment was too close," said Smokey out loud, although there was no way Danielle could hear her words in the raging gale.

Vic and Milly were sitting warm and dry when they finally delivered the sodden bed to its destination.

"Oh dear, did you get wet?" asked Milly, looking up as the women burst through the door.

Smokey and Danielle's expressions could practically kill, a fact that was lost on the simpering woman.

"Would you like a drink?" said Milly, totally unaware of her ingenuousness.

"I don't think so. We need to get back," said Smokey, pushing the fuming Danielle toward the door. "They'll learn the true meaning of 'waterbed' later tonight,'' she muttered. ''Think of that when you're climbing into your nice warm, dry four-poster.''

''Do you want some help getting this place cleaned up?'' asked Danielle. She was trying to sound sincere, but Smokey could tell she was dying to get home and change into dry clothes.

''Would you help me move the couch out? I'll vacuum and straighten things up later. I need to get started on the script.''

Five minutes later, Smokey glanced in the mirror as she was pulling on a pair of old, but warm, sweats. Her hair had frizzed up into a wild ball and her face looked washed out, with dark circles spreading under her eyes. Paul said Hank (and Cherie) wouldn't be back until Saturday, so she had all night, and maybe the morning, to repair the damage to the apartment and herself. Smokey glanced at her watch. It was already after 8:00—prime time—and she needed to get to work.

Hank arrived at her door just before midnight. Smokey looked around the cluttered living room and shuddered. Danielle had been by three hours earlier with some cold pizza, which was still sitting on the coffee table, along with several cans of diet soda.

Hank stood for a moment taking in the scene before him. ''I was hoping you would still be awake,'' he said.

He dropped his garment bag to the floor, and walked toward her. Smokey stood, as if in a trance, and found herself enfolded in his arms.

"I can't tell you how good it feels to be home," he said, his breath warm against her hair.

Home. He called this home. Smokey melted against him.

"You're early. Paul said it would be Saturday . . ."

"I couldn't wait. I took an earlier flight. I've missed you so much."

Smokey held him close, rubbing his back as he spoke. "I missed you, too," she said. "I was afraid you wouldn't come back."

"Why would you think that?"

"You've been gone so long . . . and so much has happened. You're famous, Hank Hudson. Are you sure this is where you want to be? Are you sure you won't be bored with me? My boring life? I'm not a glamorous movie star or model."

"That's such a surface existence," said Hank. "It's all based on appearance. If you're hot for the moment you can have anything you want, but if you're not hot . . . Sure, there are a lot of temptations out there. But I'm not interested."

It was exactly what Smokey wanted to hear, and she said a silent prayer of thanksgiving as she rested in his arms.

"Looks like you haven't wasted a lot of time cleaning," said Hank, taking in the food on the coffee table, the trash strewn all over the floor, and the furniture piled against the walls.

"I just moved Vic, the original 'Pigpen,' out of here," said Danielle. "I'm on deadline. Paul likes my screenplay." She looked up at him shyly.

"That's great. Way to go!" He gave her the high five.

"Yeah, but he wants all these revisions done by Monday. And every time I finish one page, I find I have to go back and redo it according to the notes on the next page. I've been working all evening, and I'm still not making much progress."

"Looks like you need an organization man," said Hank, peeling off his jacket. "Are these pages in order?"

"Pretty much," said Smokey, yawning.

"Look," said Hank. "Why don't you let me go through this thing and put together an outline of what Paul wants? It's the kind of thing I do all the time with law briefs."

"You'd do that for me?"

"Sure. It's a skill you learn inside-out in law school. Now that I don't have any classes to study for awhile, it'll be good practice for me. And it will save you a lot of time."

"Yeah, I've been feeling like I'm running around in circles."

"Okay, let's put you to bed. You look awfully tired. I'll wake you up when I'm finished."

"Really? I can go to sleep? And you'll unravel all this stuff?"

"What did you marry me for? My good looks?" Hank took her by the hand and pulled her up from the couch.

"You are kind of cute, you know," said Smokey, throwing her arms around him.

"Looks aren't everything, believe me. Even

Cherie . . .'' Hank sighed as he guided her into the bedroom. "No," he said, staring into her curious eyes. "I'll tell you all about my trip after we get this screenplay put together. You're going to get some sleep."

This wasn't exactly the homecoming she'd planned, or Hank either. But Smokey didn't waste much time thinking about it as the waves of exhaustion washed over her.

The sun was just beginning to illuminate the room when Hank slid a hot cup of coffee under Smokey's nose.

"Okay, Sleeping Beauty," he said softly. "It's my turn to make like a pumpkin."

Smokey stretched lazily, then sat up and took the coffee mug in both hands.

"I'm making pancakes. Do you want them in here or in the kitchen?"

"Better make it the kitchen," she said, rubbing her arm up and down his leg. "If I don't leave this bed soon, I may be here all day."

"No, I want you to get going on your revisions. Then we can play tonight."

"Tonight? You think I can finish that soon?"

"Definitely. Paul changed his mind on most of the revisions he suggested. Most of the things he stuck with are minor. You can rewrite with a minimum of effort. It's typical Hollywood. Change everything, and then put it back together like it was in the first place."

Smokey threw on some clothes and followed her nose to the kitchen. She stumbled into the living room and blinked twice when she surveyed the tidy scene before her. All the furniture had been moved back into place and the carpet was freshly vacuumed, the table-tops dusted. *I have to be the luckiest woman alive,* she thought. *Not only is he smart and gorgeous, he can clean and cook. Better not let this one get away, girl.*

They went through Hank's notes over breakfast and Smokey had to admit he was right. Most of Paul's changes were reversed a page later.

"You saved my life," she said. "I was in such a panic over the pages of notes, I didn't take the time to look at the big picture."

Hank looked at his watch. "You've got, let's see, until five P.M. to make all the changes. Then, you wake me up and I'll take you out for dinner. We'll put the finishing touches on the script tomorrow, and you'll be all rested and ready to go Monday morning."

"You're going to sleep for nine hours?" Smokey said to his back as he headed out the door to the bedroom.

We'll see about that, thought Smokey as she picked up Hank's notes and sat at the computer. It was suddenly all so easy, and she worked steadily for hours without a break. At 3:00, she typed the words FADE OUT and shut down the computer.

The temptation to go into the bedroom and wake Hank was overwhelming, but Smokey resolved to let him sleep. She wanted him nice and fresh for the evening. They had a lot of things to talk about, a lot of time to make up for. And now, thanks to his editing skills, she had been given the gift of time. She sat clutching her knees to her chest, savoring the peace and quiet of her little apartment. At last, she had her life back. No more Vic Cantrell, no more long-distance phone calls. She finally had Hank all to herself.

Suddenly, she remembered his comment about Cherie. What was that all about? She'd ask him later. Much later. Tonight was for the two of them, and nothing was going to interfere with that.

Chapter Fourteen

Smokey was still sitting, staring into space, an hour later when Hank emerged from the bedroom, stretching and yawning.

"Did you finish the screenplay?" he asked.

"Except for a final read-through, yes. Thanks to you. Now I'm ready to party."

"Me, too. And it's about time. Do you really think we can spend a whole evening together without anyone else showing up?"

"Yeah. What will we talk about? Without Milly or Danielle or Vic butting in?"

"I'm sure we'll think of something," said Hank, sliding onto the couch beside her and kissing her deeply.

"Mmm. Maybe we should stay in tonight," whispered Smokey.

"No way. I promised you a night on the town. It's long overdue."

"*We're* long overdue," she said, snuggling up against him.

"I hate to leave you like this, but I've got to go home and change. Let's meet back here in an hour."

"Okay. And I won't answer the door or the telephone until then."

"It's a deal."

The phone rang half an hour later, just as Smokey was emerging from the shower. *Let the machine get it,* Smokey reminded herself. "It's probably Milly calling to see if we're free to spend the evening with her and Vic," she told her reflection in the mirror.

But still she strained to hear her machine turn on. But even when she heard Danielle's voice she resisted the urge to pick up.

"Maybe I should find out what she wants," said Smokey to her reflection a few seconds after the voice ended.

Smokey hurried to the living room and hit the PLAY button on her answering machine.

"Guess you're not home." Danielle's voice stated what she clearly wished wasn't the obvious. "If you were, I'd tell you to watch 'Special Edition' on Channel Four. They're going to do a bit on Hank in a few minutes. Well, I'll record it." The phone clunked down without a good-bye.

Smokey ran to the television and skipped to Channel Four. "Hurry up," she said to the ancient set as it warmed up to where she could see the picture.

Slowly a shot of Hank emerged from the fuzz. He

was shirtless, and appeared to be tossing something, a Frisbee? to someone, a woman? Yes, it was a very beautiful young woman.

A voice-over said, "So Hollywood's latest hunk relaxes on the beach with some of his adoring fans. What's next for this up-and-coming oatmeal king? There's talk of a movie, and of course, more Elmo's Oatmeal."

The bit ended with a close-up of Hank's grinning face. Then the screen faded to a commercial.

Smokey was thoughtful as she returned to the bedroom and perched on the end of the bed. No matter how many times she saw Hank on television, no matter how many times he told her it all meant nothing, it still bothered her deeply to see him depicted as a hunk. And it especially bothered her to see him enjoying being surrounded by beautiful women. And what was this about a movie?

Just forget it, she told herself. *He's yours tonight, and you can't let anything spoil the mood. Let it go, forget about the Hollywood gossip,* she chided herself. But somehow, it just wouldn't go away, and she knew she was going to have to fight to erase that picture of him and his adoring women.

"I saw you on 'Special Edition' tonight," said Smokey later as they drove to the restaurant. "Did you know you were going to be featured?" Smokey didn't like the whiny note in her voice, but she couldn't help herself.

"No, what was I doing?"

"Playing catch with a beautiful model. When was that?"

"A bunch of us were messing around at the studio one day weeks ago, and the cameras were there taking pictures. It was no big deal."

"They said you were at the beach."

"That proves it. We were on a set made up to look like the ocean. Amazing, isn't it?"

"Yeah, amazing," said Smokey. *What is wrong with you?* she asked herself as they drove on in silence. *Most women would be thrilled to be dating a Hollywood hunk. But I'm not most women,* she told herself. *I just want a nice quiet relationship without other women chasing after my man. I finally found someone who truly makes me happy. Why do I keep feeling like he's slipping away from me?*

Don't be silly, she told herself. *There's real chemistry between us, and Hank's not going to let all this publicity go to his head.*

"What do you tell reporters when they ask if you're married?" asked Smokey, hating her words the moment she spoke them.

"I try to avoid that topic," said Hank. "If they would check my background, there's no documentation for a marriage. I don't want to be caught in a lie. I figure if I stay away from it, it will just be part of my mystique."

"I suppose," said Smokey unhappily. "I guess we're both in a bind on this one."

"Hey, look over there," said Hank, braking the car. He was pointing down the street.

Smokey peered out the window at a huge billboard

hovering over them. A giant Hank stood full length wearing tight jeans and a blue T-shirt. One hand rested on his waist, the other held a box of Elmo's Oatmeal. ''Oh, wow,'' said Smokey. ''You look like Paul Bunyan.''

''It is a little intimidating, isn't it? I had no idea it was going to be so big.''

''It is that,'' said Smokey. ''Big.'' *And women all over California are going to be slobbering over that billboard every day. But he's mine. I don't want to share him.*

Things got worse when they arrived at the restaurant. Chi Su's was an unassuming café with a reputation for the best Chinese food in Southern California. It was one of those ''finds'' that the locals tried to keep to themselves so that it wouldn't be spoiled by hordes of tourists. But on this night it was obvious that the secret was out, and a line of hungry people had formed outside the door.

''Saturday night,'' said Smokey. ''Remember when you could walk in Chi Su's anytime and immediately get a table?''

''Yeah, the good old days,'' said Hank, sliding into a parking place and grabbing her hand as they walked down the street.

Smokey noticed a murmuring as they strolled along the sidewalk, but it wasn't until they took their place at the end of the line that it became obvious something was going on. Glancing down the row, Smokey noticed everyone was staring at them.

''You're the guy from the oatmeal commercial, aren't you?'' said the woman closest to them. ''I can't believe it. It's him!'' she yelled, and soon women from half a block away were crowding around them, touching Hank, begging for his autograph.

Smokey found herself pushed up against the wall as the crowd surged around her. *This is insane,* she thought as she was shoved out of the way, losing sight of Hank as the knot of women swelled around him.

''Smokey!'' She heard him call out her name, but she couldn't see him in the mass of humanity swirling around her. ''Meet me at the car.''

It was easy for Smokey to work her way back up the street. No one cared about her. But it was another twenty minutes before Hank came jogging toward her.

''Quick,'' he called. ''Get in the car.''

He was panting, and Smokey noticed his shirt was torn, and several buttons were missing.

''The price of fame,'' he said as soon as they were safely in the car with the doors locked.

They were both silent as they drove back to the apartment. Their life together had changed drastically in those few minutes, and they both knew it, but neither of them had any idea how they were going to deal with it.

''I guess we'll have to order a pizza after all,'' said Hank when they pulled into the parking lot. He smiled sadly at Smokey as he followed her into her apartment.

''We don't value our freedom until we lose it, do we?'' said Smokey.

''No, and I've been learning that on a daily basis. I guess it's time I hired a bodyguard like Paul suggested.''

"A bodyguard? Are you serious? Talk about losing your freedom."

"Goes with the territory."

"It sounds like you plan on this continuing for a while."

"What? The celebrity trip? Probably." Hank refused to look her in the eye.

"They were talking about a possible movie on television tonight."

"We're considering it."

"What about law school?"

"It'll keep. I'm making more money than I ever could practicing law, Smokey. I can't just turn my back on an opportunity like this."

"Money isn't everything. You worked so hard to get this far. I can't believe you're going to give it all up," said Smokey.

"You just don't understand, do you?"

"I understand how exciting it all must be. I understand how a person could get lost in the world of Hollywood glitter. But I also understand that I couldn't live that kind of life."

"What are you saying, Smokey?" Hank's eyes had narrowed and he had pulled back from her.

"I'm saying that I need my privacy. And most of all, I need a man who I know is going to be there for me on a daily basis, not someone I see on television surrounded by beautiful women."

"Are you telling me to get lost?"

"No, I'm telling you that maybe we met each other at the wrong time. I fell for a guy who I hardly recognize anymore, a guy whose values have changed before my very eyes. I don't want to be your 'down-to-earth, no-frills' woman, Hank. I just want to be your woman, the only woman in your life.''

"Well, I guess there's not much more I can say. I'm not going to pass up these opportunities."

"And I'm not going to ask you to. I'm just saying I can't handle your lifestyle."

"Just because a bunch of women attacked me?"

"No. Because you're a different person now. I've been here for the last few months, handling my job, Vic Cantrell, Milly, and watching you posing with starlets, a different one every night. I need someone who's got his feet on the ground, who's going to be there for me, not gallivanting around the country."

Smokey didn't like her words, but they just came out. She'd been holding it all in too long, and now all her anger and resentment came pouring out and she couldn't stop.

"It's all smoke and mirrors and you know it," said Hank. "The photographers get what they want and interpret it their way. You can't take it seriously."

"And what about law school? Was that all smoke and mirrors, too? Here you are, signing on for a movie. Another semester of school delayed. This is going to be your life, isn't it? The glamour, the girls, the meaningless dalliances. This isn't a temporary moneymaker anymore, is it? You love the attention, the glory of it all."

"Sure, I've enjoyed it. No one in their right mind would say they didn't. But I also know it's temporary. I'm just taking advantage of an opportunity while it's available. Law school will always be there."

Smokey looked at him in disgust, and he got up without a word and headed for the door. Then he stopped, and looked back at her sitting in her misery.

"And what I didn't tell you about Cherie? She's been after me from day one. She's done everything but stand on her head to get me romantically involved with her. You were right about her, Smokey. But you were wrong about me. I wasn't even tempted."

Chapter Fifteen

By Monday morning, Smokey felt good about the script she carried into Paul Girard's office. Losing herself in the final editing process had been her salvation on Sunday, the only thing that could possibly keep her from thinking about Hank and the terrible things they had said to each other the night before.

And on this morning, as she watched Paul skim through the pages, a smile of approval on his face, she couldn't help but think how ironic it was that Hank was more than partially responsible for making it a far better screenplay than it had been the week before. He had been such an important part of her life in so many ways, it was difficult for her to accept the fact that he was gone so quickly.

Ironic, too, was the subject of the screenplay. It was the story of Peg, a young woman from Iowa who moved to New York and found success in the fashion industry. The character was perhaps too close to reality for Smokey. But it was Hank who helped her develop the woman's role, adding spice to her dialogue and heating up the love scenes with her erstwhile boyfriend, whom she eventually rejected in a dramatic scene of discovery and independence.

Art imitating life once again, she thought, reliving once again the horrible mob scene at the Chinese restaurant, and the argument afterward. *But I had to stand up for what I believe. I had to let him know I thought he was making a mistake.*

The day Smokey learned her script had been sold was the same day Hank signed to star in his own movie. Not that he called to tell her the news. She read about it in the newspaper, which she wadded up and threw in the trash after staring at the picture of him with his beautiful costar, the two of them standing with their arms around each other, beaming at the camera.

She resigned her position with Tri-Arts that day, and hired Paul to represent her in the final negotiations. Several people stopped by to congratulate her as she was packing up her desk, and without fail, each mentioned Hank's success.

"A real power couple, you two," said April, the receptionist. "Guess you've got the world by the tail."

There was no longer any need to maintain the marriage ruse, but Smokey didn't have the energy to go into explanations. She just smiled sadly and left the office without fanfare.

*   *   *

"So why am I not happy?" said Smokey as she and Danielle celebrated over hot-fudge sundaes at the Ice Cream Palace. "I've finally got everything I wanted. Almost."

"You're asking the wrong person," said Danielle. "I'd kill to be a star."

"Did you see Hank on 'Show Buzz' last night?" Smokey wasn't even listening to Danielle.

"Yeah. I wasn't going to mention it."

"That's the third starlet he's been linked with in the last few weeks," said Smokey.

"That doesn't mean anything. It's all publicity."

"Maybe. But how many men could resist that temptation? And how many women could sit by and watch their man in that situation?"

"I don't know. I guess if it were me, I'd be in there ripping that bimbo's hair out."

"But that's not me, Danielle. I just sit home and suffer. I don't want to live like that."

"Maybe he'll come to his senses. You two were so good together."

"We were, weren't we?" Tears were welling in Smokey's eyes. "But I'm afraid it's just too late."

The production company that had picked up the option on Smokey's screenplay was begging her to come to Phoenix to help with the rewrite. She had resisted, insisting that she needed to stay in Los Angeles to complete the new screenplay she was working on. But now, she had lost her enthusiasm for writing. Her creativity had run dry, and she spent her days pacing the floor, feeling like a caged animal. Everything in the apartment, everything in her life, reminded her of Hank. And to make matters worse, she saw his face again and again on television and in magazines. He was the toast of Hollywood, and Smokey could hardly bear to get up in the morning and face each new day.

"This is insane!" she cried to Danielle. "I've dreamed of the day I could afford to write full-time. And now I can't sit still."

Danielle shook her head. Smokey was very much aware that their friendship was suffering because of her angst. Danielle and Nick were enjoying a great relationship, but Danielle was uncomfortable talking about it, because her best friend didn't want to hear all the romantic details.

"Maybe you should think about going to Arizona," said Danielle. "I'd miss you terribly. But it might be good for you."

"Maybe I should. I'm not accomplishing anything, sitting around here."

"Do it. You'll be busy and maybe you'll be able to get your mind off the Oatmeal Man."

Smokey left for Phoenix two days later, and by the next morning, she was locked in a room with the six other writers hired to polish the script. After that, her schedule never varied, as the group struggled to re-work the words she had written to satisfy the whims of the temperamental staff who was producing the script. They worked long hours, six days a week, and on the seventh day Smokey retired to her hotel room and slept around the clock.

In between naps she called Danielle, asking about

her movie, but hoping she had some news about Hank.
Finally, one week she did.

"I saw him driving a new sports car last week,"
said Danielle. "Very hip and very expensive."

"He gave up Susie Subaru? He loved that car."

"I guess so."

"Did he have a woman with him?"

"Nope. He was alone."

"Good," said Smokey. "I mean, I don't care. I
just . . ."

"Yeah, I know," said Danielle.

The next weekend, Danielle called her on Sunday
morning, waking her from a sound sleep.

"How's it going?" asked Danielle.

"Miserable. It's a lousy job, but it keeps me busy.
I haven't seen a newspaper in weeks."

"Then you haven't heard."

"Heard what?"

"It may mean nothing, but I just read it in *Variety*."

"What?" Smokey had a feeling this was going to
be about Hank, and she was steeling herself for the
worst.

"Hank. He walked off his movie set. No real explanation. The paper said there were 'artistic
differences.' "

"I wonder what that means. Maybe he didn't get
the dressing room he wanted."

"Come on, Smokey. That doesn't sound like
Hank."

"No, it doesn't. I wonder . . ."

"I'll keep my ear to the ground. See what I can find out."

"Okay," said Smokey thoughtfully. She hated to hear about Hank, but she couldn't stand *not* hearing about him.

"So, when are you coming home?"

"I don't know. I really miss my little apartment, my little life, and . . ."

"I know, I know. I miss having you around. Although Nick and I aren't too exciting these days. The movie comes out in a month and we just sit around chewing our nails. Wish you were here to share our fun."

Smokey hung up the phone, a whole new cloud of depression hanging over her. She wanted desperately to go home, but she needed more time. More time to forget about him . . . the Oatmeal Man.

By the end of the fifth week, the script had been rewritten five times, and it was starting to resemble the original screenplay Smokey had submitted many months earlier. She was quickly losing her enthusiasm for the project in spite of the excellent money they were paying her.

That weekend she called Danielle. "I'm tired, lonely, and depressed," she said. "I want to come home."

"Then you should," said her friend. "After all, you can be all those things here. Except you won't have to pay long-distance rates to tell me about it."

"Okay. I'll make my reservations tomorrow. With a little luck, I'll be back in L.A. by next weekend."

Smokey heaved a sigh of relief. Just the thought of going home raised her spirits. She needed to be surrounded by her things, her friends—even Milly and Vic sounded like fun at this point. Getting over Hank wasn't going to be easy wherever she was, but time and good friends would help.

"Great!" said Danielle. "I'm going to plan a party for the next weekend, so don't you dare back out on me."

"I don't want a party, Danielle."

"Yes, you do. You'll see!"

Nick and Danielle were at the airport to meet her, and Smokey cried when she hugged her best friend.

"More crying," said Nick. "Danielle's been sniffling all morning."

"What's the matter? Is something wrong?"

"No," said Danielle. "The first reviews are just starting to come in. And . . ."

"And?" said Smokey, expecting the worst.

"And they're great! I'm getting all kinds of offers! And now, my best friend is back, and everything's so wonderful!"

"Oh, Danielle! I'm so happy for you."

"She's missed you," said Nick. "I'm glad you're back."

"Me, too," said Smokey. "I guess sometimes you have to go away to realize how important your friends are." She was starting to tear up.

"It's just so scary," said Danielle, starting to lose it.

"What?" said Smokey.

"I'm just so afraid. Afraid it's all going to end overnight. Life's so weird. Like you and Hank . . ."

"Oh, Danielle." Now Smokey was definitely crying.

"I give up," said Nick. "You two are going to drive me crazy."

"I'll be good," said Danielle, flinging her arms over both their shoulders. "Besides, I'll be busy with Smokey's party next weekend. I won't have time to think about the movie, and life in general."

"But I don't want a party—" said Smokey.

"Shhh," said Nick. "Do us all a favor and go along with it. Please."

Smokey shook her head. This obviously wasn't going to be a battle she could win.

Chapter Sixteen

"Okay. I'll go to the party," said Smokey at the end of the week. "But can't I at least see the guest list?"

"Nope. It's all going to be a surprise. Trust me. All your friends will be there."

Smokey sighed. "I don't have that many friends."

"So, it's a small party," said Danielle brightly.

"What should I wear?"

"Something simple and innocent. A sundress maybe."

"Innocent? What's going on, Danielle? Level with me, or I'm not going to show up."

"Nothing. Honest," said Danielle, her eyes opened wide. "But you're the guest of honor, and I want you to look beautiful. We've celebrated my success, we even celebrated Hank's success. And now it's time for you to get a little recognition. The plans have already been made and the invitations sent. You can't back out on me now.''

''I wish you wouldn't do this, Danielle. You know how I hate these scenes. Especially now.''

''Humor me, Smokey. You know how I'm addicted to parties. Do this for me.''

Although she never would have admitted it to Danielle, by the night of the party, Smokey was almost looking forward to going. The depression of sitting in her apartment every day, staring at the blank computer screen, was starting to take its toll. She was secretly looking forward to having people make a fuss over her. It was her turn after all.

As always when she went anywhere with Danielle, they were late getting started and they arrived at the party almost an hour after it was supposed to start. Even at that the festivities were just getting under way at the hotel party room Danielle had rented for the evening. Paul Girard and his wife were just arriving, as was a beaming Milly, supporting Vic in his walking cast.

Smokey was forced to listen to Vic's complaints and Milly's giggling and didn't even notice the sign on the wall until she was in the middle of the room. And even then, she didn't get it. Over and over, she read the words sparkling in huge letters. HAPPY UN-WEDDING, HANK AND SMOKEY!

There was a look of horror on her face as she turned to find Danielle and demand an explanation. Instead, she came nose to nose with Hank, who was also staring at the sign.

''Was this your idea?'' he said under his breath as

Danielle strode to the microphone at the front of the room.

Smokey shook her head, unable to speak. She wanted to grab Danielle somehow and stop her from opening her mouth, but it was too late.

"Whereas, these two people were joined in unholy matrimony, under completely false circumstances." Danielle's voice blared over the loudspeaker as she pointed at Hank and Smokey. "And whereas, we are gathered here tonight here tonight to expose this bogus marriage, let the unwed couple step forward to finalize this ruse they have been putting over on all of you."

Hank and Smokey were pushed to the front of the room, and an actor dressed as a priest stepped forward.

"By the power vested in me by the wardrobe department of Gemstone Studios, I now pronounce you nonhusband and nonwife. All you men may kiss the unbride, and all you women may kiss the ungroom."

Smokey looked helplessly at Hank as they were both deluged with well-wishers.

Rock-and-roll music poured from the speakers as Smokey found herself passed from partner to partner in a frenzy of craziness on the dance floor. Hank, too, had a line of women waiting to sashay across the floor with him. In spite of the smile plastered on his face, he would search her eyes whenever they passed, as if looking for some kind of sign.

"Well, you pulled one over on me," said Paul Girard, when he commandeered Smokey for one of the reasonably slow dances. "Danielle told me about the job interview. That's just the kind of creative mind

I was looking for. I think I would have hired you anyway. I know talent when I see it.''

''Now you tell me,'' said Smokey.

''And now I'm without an editorial assistant again. I think I'll have you and Danielle screen the next batch of applicants.''

''Be happy to,'' said Smokey. ''But wearing a wedding ring wouldn't be one of my requirements.''

Paul Girard was still laughing when he felt a tap on his shoulder. He twirled Smokey around and passed her into Hank's waiting arms without missing a beat.

''Don't I know you from somewhere?'' said Hank.

''I think we had a thing once,'' said Smokey, fitting comfortably into his embrace.

''It's so hard to make a relationship work in these turbulent times. What with all the pressures of society.''

''Fame and fortune don't help, either,'' she said.

''No, it's all an illusion, isn't it? But in the end we're all alone.''

''I don't think you'll ever be alone, Mr. Oatmeal Man. If only half of your press coverage is accurate, you won't be lonely for long.''

''You really believe all those tabloid stories?''

''I saw you. . . . Every time I picked up a magazine or turned on the TV, there you were, kissing someone new, some vapid little starlet.''

''Did you ever see me kiss the same one twice?''

''No. You think *that* makes it better?''

''Smokey, don't you see? It was all publicity. Plain and simple. Every time I turned around they had someone standing there waiting to pose.''

"But it doesn't do much for a relationship."

"Well, that's all over now," said Hank.

"What do you mean?"

"There you are!" said Danielle loudly, as she appeared out of nowhere. "Time to cut the cake."

"Cake?" they said in unison.

"Cakes, actually. One for each of you. No more sharing. Now you can have your cake and eat it, too."

Once again all eyes were focused on Hank and Smokey as Danielle dragged them again to the front of the room, where two cakes—one chocolate, one vanilla—stood waiting.

"I think it would be real cute if you'd each cut a piece and then throw it at each other," whispered Danielle. "You know, sort of symbolic of the end of the marriage."

"I don't think . . ." said Smokey.

"Good idea," said Hank, a twinkle in his eye.

There was a drum roll while they stood, backs to each other, cutting their cakes. Then they turned and stood still. Hank hesitated, then extended his hand as if offering Smokey a bite. The next moment the chocolate cake came propelling toward her, smashing her face and cascading down the front of her pale pink dress.

Smokey looked down at the mess before pulling her arm back and hurling her white cake at his chest. A huge roar went up from the audience gathered around the little stage.

Hank grabbed another chunk of cake and threw it at the audience, and Smokey quickly followed suit, managing to hit Milly Edwards right in the center of her open mouth. In seconds a full-fledged food fight broke out. People were screaming and cake was flying. In the midst of all the turmoil, Hank grabbed Smokey's hand and pulled her off to a corner with a sign marked EXIT.

"Mob mentality at its best," he said. "It works every time. Let's get out of here."

"But the party. We're the guests of honor."

"They won't even miss us. They're all too busy getting their pent-up aggressions out. That's why they all came in the first place. To celebrate the end of a relationship. They love it when other people are unhappy. It makes their own miserable lives more bearable."

"Where are we going?" said Smokey.

"Out of here. Someplace where we can talk."

People stared at them as they crossed the lobby, both shedding globs of cake and frosting with each step.

"We just got divorced," said Smokey to an over-dressed society matron who stopped in their path and glared at them.

"I don't think she appreciates the humor of our state of matrimony," whispered Hank as they maneuvered a big circle around the indignant woman.

"Well, this is certainly a lot more fun than my last divorce," said Smokey.

"Mine, too."

They had arrived at the front door of the hotel, and Hank handed the valet his ticket.

"Aren't you . . . ?" said the valet, staring at Hank.

"Nope. It's not me," said Hank. "My car, please. It's a metallic tan Subaru. A classic."

"Susie Subaru?" said Smokey. "But Danielle said you bought a new sports car."

"I did. But I missed Susie, so I bought her back."

"You're kidding!"

"I've still got the sports car. I just don't drive it very often."

"Where are we going?" asked Smokey once the valet was tipped and they were on their way.

"Not too many places we can go looking like this. How about your apartment? I have a new place, but I'm not unpacked yet. And what little space I might have is covered with cases of Elmo's Oatmeal."

"Are you still filming commercials for them?"

"Nope. That first one ran its course. The later ones just didn't match up. I was a one-commercial wonder. The company kissed me off with a lifetime supply of oatmeal."

"And your movie?"

"I walked out. They're probably going to sue me."

"What happened?"

"They neglected to tell me my part included extensive location work in Siberia. When I discovered that, I knew my days as a movie star were over."

"You're kidding! They wanted you to work out there?"

"Yep. That's when I decided I'd rather be a lawyer than a popsicle."

"So?"

"So I'm going back to school next semester. I've been meeting with my old study group just to keep current, prepare for the bar exams. And I do some pro bono work at a free legal clinic downtown.''

''That's great, Hank. I'm glad you made that decision.''

''Me, too. You were right, you know. It took me a while to figure it out, but I'm glad I did.''

''And Cherie Howe?''

''History . . . I should have gotten rid of her long before I did. I guess my male ego enjoyed having her around.''

They sat silently for a few moments, both of them trying to decide what to say next.

''I've missed you, Smokey. More than I ever thought I would.''

''Oh, Hank. Me, too.''

''So do you think we could start over? Try to get it right this time? I mean, I don't have much to offer. I'm a has-been hunk with no job, a lawsuit hanging over my head, an old beat-up car, and a lot of oatmeal. But I promise I'll never let you down again. I'll always be there for you.''

''I really don't care about all that other stuff. But a lifetime supply of oatmeal . . . well, that's pretty appealing. I guess I'd be willing to give it a try.''

They had arrived at the parking lot of Smokey's apartment building. Hank pulled Susie Subaru into a slot, then turned and took Smokey in his arms, his eyes sparkling with joy.

''We never had that night on the town,'' said Hank finally. ''Want to hit the hot spots tonight?''

''All I'd like to do right now is get rid of this sticky cake and put on some comfortable clothes.''

''Me, too. How about I cook? You've never tasted my Steak à la Hudson.''

''Sounds heavenly. But what if Milly comes by? Or Danielle?''

''I'll fix enough for everyone. The more the merrier. Just promise me you'll be there when everyone leaves.''

''I will.''

''Forever?''

Smokey nodded happily.

DATE DUE

RCW			
MM			

Charlotte County Library
P.O. Box 788
Charlotte C.H., VA 23923

DEMCO